THE RUTHENIAN LITURGY

An Historical-Theoretical Explication

The Ruthenian Liturgy

Statement

The Ruthenian Rite's Greek origins and distinctively Slavonic character ground this analysis of the revised Divine Liturgy, promulgated in 2007 by The Byzantine Metropolitan Church *Sui Juris* of Pittsburgh, U.S.A. Despite a few improvements, the revision is theologically and musically inferior to what had been in use since the 1970s.

THE RUTHENIAN LITURGY
An Historical-Theoretical Explication

Catherine Brown Tkacz

With a Foreword by
Jeffrey Burton Russell

The Edwin Mellen Press
Lewiston•Queenston•Lampeter

Library of Congress Cataloging-in-Publication Data

Tkacz, Catherine Brown.
  The Ruthenian liturgy : an historical-theological explication / Catherine Tkacz ; with a foreword by Jeffrey Burton Russell.
    p. cm.
  Includes bibliographical references and index.
  ISBN-13: 978-0-7734-2555-2 (hardcover)
  ISBN-10: 0-7734-2555-1 (hardcover)
1. Ruthenian Catholic Church--Liturgy. I. Title.
  BX4711.963.T43 2011
  264'.0152--dc23

                       2011045376

hors série.

A CIP catalog record for this book is available from the British Library.

The Edwin Mellen Press   The Edwin Mellen Press
Box 450   Box 67
Lewiston, New York   Queenston, Ontario
USA 14092-0450   CANADA L0S 1L0

The Edwin Mellen Press, Ltd.
Lampeter, Ceredigion, Wales
UNITED KINGDOM SA48 8LT

Printed in the United States of America

Ut unum sint.

The Ruthenian Liturgy
Abstract

The Ruthenian Rite is the Slavonic version of Greek Catholicism, brought to the Slavs in the ninth century by SS. Cyril and Methodius. In America the Ruthenian Catholic Church is The Byzantine Metropolitan Church *Sui Juris* of Pittsburgh, U.S.A. Since the 1970s its liturgy has often been celebrated in English. In 2007 a much revised liturgy with myriad changes in language and music was promulgated. Analyzed in the context of the Ruthenian Rite and Greek Catholicism, the revised liturgy is shown to have a few excellent changes, such as substituting "Covenant" for "Testament" in the anaphora. Overall, however, the revision is deeply flawed.

The right of the faithful to authentic liturgy has been affirmed in the document *Liturgiam Authenticam*. For Ruthenians the authoritative Slavonic liturgy is to be respected; that is, the Slavonic is not to be scanted in favor of the Greek. For instance, whereas the Greek liturgy describes the bishop as Θεοφιλεστάτου (*theophilestatou*), which can mean either "[most] God-loving" or "whom God loves [greatly]," the Slavonic unambiguously has ъоҍолюҍивім (*bohol'ubiv'im*) "God-loving," and so that meaning ought to be used in any English version of the Ruthenian liturgy. A special case is the word Θεοτόκος (*Theotokos*). As a new word study shows, this distinctive title for Mary literally means "Birth of God," and it was translated into Slavonic as *Bohoróditsa*. It is not clear that the venerable Slavonic term *Bohoróditsa* ought to be absent from the Ruthenian Rite in English, in favor of the Greek term *Theotokos*.

The Ruthenian Rite is itself contemplative, coherent, inspired, focused on theosis (divinization or sanctification), and affirmative of women. The Christian emphasis on the spiritual equality of the sexes has been dynamically shown from the New Testament onwards. A doctrinal program of the balance of the sexes is seen in, for instance, Ruthenian liturgical hymns and the Church calendar. In contrast, the secularizing language imposed in the revised Divine Liturgy – such as cutting the word "men" from the Symbolum (Creed) – resulted in a text with a limited shelf life. Idiosyncratic new translations such as "Holy gifts for holy people" needlessly distance Ruthenian worship from the Orthodox.

Liturgical music is itself theologically shaped and expresses worship, as shown by an analysis of Slavonic chant. Countless changes in the music are in the sum distracting from worship, and in several cases are seen to have been made without a full understanding of what the original chant was accomplishing. In addition, a survey of Slavonic paraliturgical communion hymns and carols shows that the revised Divine Liturgy inappropriately introduced the use of nonliturgical melodies for the Cherubikon and other liturgical texts.

Access to the contents of the book, including its numerous word studies, is enhanced by comprehensive indices: general, scriptural, and for each pertinent language.

Table of Contents

Acknowledgments

My husband, Dr. Michael W. Tkacz, by marriage and character and intellect gave me deep Byzantine roots. The support and devoted interest of my fellow parishioners at SS. Cyril and Methodius Byzantine Catholic Church in Spokane, Washington, were invaluable: often they voiced well-informed remarks about the revised Divine Liturgy of March 25, 2005, some of which are cited below. For the excellent work of Mr. John Vernoski in the presentation and analysis of authentic Byzantine chant I am most grateful, having had the strong joy of worshipping for several years with his settings, prior to the promulgation of the revised *Divine Liturgy*. The spiritual direction and learned conversation of Rev. Paul S. Vevik of the Diocese of Spokane was a helpful stimulus throughout the writing of this book. Several priests, Byzantine Catholic, Roman Catholic and Orthodox, and a number of seminarians of the Bishop White Seminary at Gonzaga University in Spokane, Washington, have likewise encouraged this research. Professor Jeffrey Burton Russell is primary among the colleagues who have discussed it with me and insightfully critiqued parts or all of this book, much to my benefit.

Some of the research underlying this book was conducted in Washington, D.C., at the Dominican House of Studies, Dumbarton Oaks, and The Catholic University of America; and at Oxford University at the Bodleian Library and at Blackfriars Hall. The word Θεοφιλεστάτος was the object of my research using the Thesaurus Linguae Graecae, conducted at the University of Notre Dame while my husband and I were there for the annual meeting of the American Catholic Philosophical Association in 2005. I am grateful to the National Endowment for the Humanities for research grants which funded aspects of my research drawn upon in this book. Both the Dominican House of Studies in Washington, D.C., and Blackfriars Hall at Oxford University have graciously extended their hospitality to me during research trips.

Foreword

By Professor Jeffrey Burton Russell

Catherine Brown Tkacz is one of the best living scholars in Biblical studies, Latin patristics, and medieval theology and liturgy, to which she brings a strong working knowledge of Latin, Greek, German, Slavonic, and French. Her work is characterized by deep understanding of texts, artworks, and musicology. Her writing is splendid: she is a published poet as well as the author of many scholarly books and articles, and she has an extraordinary sensitivity to the connotations of words in many languages. Her recent research into the Book of Daniel and its relation to the New Testament Passion narratives is a landmark in New Testament studies; she is also a leading scholar of typology, which was important in Christian thinking up into the nineteenth century but then neglected until she helped revive it in the last decade of the twentieth.

Her new book, *The Ruthenian Liturgy,* is not only an important contribution to Eastern Christian theology and liturgy; it also has great bearing on all traditional churches, including those in the West. It emphasizes the importance of the Slavonic as well as other liturgical traditions. Its happy and also carefully critical celebration of Eastern-rite Catholicism should help bring reconciliation and unity among all apostolic churches closer. All Christians need to honor the diversity of authentic rites within the unity of the Church. An understanding of the variety of authentic traditions in the Catholic and Orthodox Churches will move us all toward charitable reunion in Christ, especially important today when all of Christianity is under renewed attack by atheists and secularists.

The book discusses the changes made in the Ruthenian Liturgy in America during the period 2005-2007. Dr. Tkacz welcomes some of the changes promulgated in January 2007 while discussing the problems inherent in other changes and suggesting the further improvements that are still essential to be made. Her brilliant section "Principles for Liturgical Translation and Revision" points out that changes must be an improvement. Changes must be rooted in the theology, text, and music of the traditional church; they must help the liturgy become both more precise and deeper; they must avoid banal dumbing down; they must avoid confusing the faithful by unnecessary alterations of words and rhythms. For example, in Western Churches since the 1960s a number of different translations of the "Our Father" were introduced, with the result that many people are so confused that they are unsure how to say it.

Important to all Christians are other points in the book:

It is crucially necessary to understand and translate the Old Testament in accordance with its most ancient documents, which are in Greek (the Septuagint, the translation of Theodotion, and other Old Greek texts). In most cases, the most authoritative Old Testament texts are pre-Christian Greek. Most modern translations rely too heavily on the Hebrew, which in most cases is later than the Greek and which contains demonstrable changes in the text made for the purpose of opposing Christianity. Roman Catholic and, especially, Protestant Bibles pay too little attention to the importance of the early Greek. A new translation of the Old Testament that takes the Greek as a strong foundation would be of enormous value.

Understanding of Mary as Christ-Bearer is deepened by the author's exploration of the terms *Theotokos, Deipara, Theogenesia, Mater Dei*, and *Bohoróditsa*. Her suggestion of "Birth of God" as a valid translation is worth consideration. On the whole, women were vastly more important in both the Old and the New Testaments than has been acknowledged by most scholars since 1970. What may be called the "Old Feminism," the effort to minimize the importance of women in Christianity for political purposes in order to attack misogyny, is now being replaced by the "New Feminism," the demonstration of the enormous importance of women both in the Bible and in traditional Christian liturgy. This point is one on which Dr. Tkacz's work has been most extensive and magisterial. Her recent publications make the point with such scrupulous thoroughness and care that the point can no longer be disputed by any honest and well-informed scholar. The New Feminism puts research and facts above propaganda.

A related important section deals with the term "man" in the Bible, the Creeds, and tradition. The simplest, yet least tractable, problem is the meaning of the word "man" in English. Greek, Latin, and German have a word for "human being" in general as well as words for the separate genders. Until the 1960s, everyone understood that in English "man" is often generic:

Charles Darwin published *The Descent of Man* and the Communist Internationale sang of the brotherhood of man. Since then, politics have forced us away from simple and elegant usage. Whether this is good or bad I do not presume to declare, but "He became human" may be a good temporary solution until the language improves.

This knowledgeable, precise, thorough, calm, and authoritative book needs to be read by all persons of all traditional churches with a deep interest in theology and liturgy. Its importance goes far beyond what its title modestly indicates.

Jeffrey Burton Russell
Professor of History, Emeritus
University of California

Prologue

Rare is the opportunity to view an event from two perspectives, both anticipating what it would be like were it to happen, and also seeing what its effects are when it has in fact occurred. The present volume allows such a twofold vantage point on the revised Divine Liturgy, promulgated in 2007 for the Ruthenian Catholic Church in the United States. The formal name of this church is The Byzantine Catholic Metropolitan Church *Sui Juris* of Pittsburgh, USA. This book assesses the theological and pastoral issues raised between 2005, when the draft revision was issued, and 2007, when the revised liturgy was promulgated. It also discusses the subsequent effects of the new liturgy.

In April 2005 I wrote a detailed analysis of the draft revision and provided a copy to each of our hierarchs. My parish priest asked permission to put my essay on our parish's website, and I readily agreed. After an Eastern Catholic priest in Europe read my analysis online, he and the managing editor of an Eastern Catholic press asked me to expand it into a monograph. I delivered the resulting book some months later. Regrettably, although the manuscript had reached the stage of final proofs with full index more than three years ago, the press experienced financial difficulties and did not actually print the book. Meanwhile, the revised liturgy was promulgated in January 2007 and became mandatory for use as of June 29, 2007. The new liturgy was published as *The Divine Liturgies of Our Holy Fathers John Chrysostom and Basil the Great: Responses and Hymns set to the Carpathian Plainchant* (Pittsburgh: The Byzantine Catholic Metropolitan Church *Sui Juris* of Pittsburgh, USA, 2006).

The present book contains my full analysis, with its copious reference to the 2005 liturgy issued specifically for March 25, 2005, and with detailed citations of the drafts of the revised Divine Liturgy as they existed in 2004 - 2006. The present volume also supplements that full analysis in three ways. First, works that were then "forthcoming" are now cited in full, with date of publication and page numbers. Second, frequent reference is now made to the promulgated form of the revised Divine Liturgy. These comments are enclosed in square brackets [] so that the line of the original argument of the book remains intact. Third, this prologue and an epilogue have been added.

May the present volume stand as an affirmation of the strength, beauty, coherence, and theological profundity of authentic Ruthenian worship specifically and of the Divine Liturgy in every tradition.

Original Introduction

At the start of the third millennium Ruthenian Catholics and indeed all Eastern Catholics have entrusted to us the mission of being the Orientale Lumen within the Catholic Church. Fittingly, this mission is three-part. This mission is to serve those who are Eastern Catholic and who need and have the right to worship in their authentic traditions. This mission is also to serve those who are Roman Catholic and who need and have a right to our fraternal example of distinctively Eastern worship, a worship which, in many ways, expresses more fully the doctrines of theosis or divinization and of the spiritual equality of women than is the case in current American practice of the Roman rite.[1] And this mission is to serve the Orthodox as well: As the Churches approach the sad millennium of the Schism, we Eastern Catholics are to honor and worship in the liturgy we share with the Orthodox, so that we may be an incarnate invitation for renewed unity in the Church, and, equally, so that we may respond rightly to the invitation for renewed unity which the Orthodox incarnate. In the words of Patriarch Maximos IV of Antioch, articulating "The Eastern Role in Christian Reunion," we are "to remain at the same time profoundly Catholic and profoundly Eastern."[2]

The several Eastern Catholic Churches include the Greek Catholic, the Syro-Malabarese Catholic, the Ethiopian Catholic, and the Maronite Catholic, for instance. The designation "Greek Catholic" points to the primacy of the Greek Scriptures and liturgies for these Churches. Even though the Slavs, for instance, translated the Septuagint into Slavonic, it was the Greek, not the Hebrew that they translated.[3] (Of this, more below.) Although the mission of SS. Cyril and Methodius likewise rendered into Slavonic the Divine Liturgy of St. John Chrysostom and other Greek liturgies and proper hymn-texts, the underlying commonality of the Greek Churches is in their recognition of the authority of the pre-Christian Jewish Greek version of the Old Testament and it is also in their shared worship in rites initially composed in Greek.

---

[1] For a developed discussion of this topic, incorporating much secondary literature by Orthodox scholars, see Catherine Brown Tkacz, "Women and the Church in the New Millennium," *Saint Vladimir's Theological Quarterly* 52.3-4 (2008) 243-74.

[2] Conference given in Düsseldorf, 9 August 1960, *Prôche-Orient chrétien* 10 (Jerusalem, 1960): 291-302; English translation in *The Eastern Churches and Catholic Unity* (Freiburg: Herder; and Edinburgh-London: Nelson, 1963), 46-61, quotation from p. 56, cited and English translation corrected by Serge Keleher, "Ukrainian Catholics: Four Translations of the Divine Liturgy, Some Early Translations," *Logos: A Journal of Eastern Christian Studies* 39.2-4 (1998): 267-402, at 296-97.

[3] See, e.g., Horace G. Lunt and Moshe Taube, *The Slavonic Book of Esther: Text, Lexicon, Linguistic Analysis, Problems of Translating,* Harvard Series in Ukrainian Studies (Cambridge: Harvard University Press for the Harvard Ukrainian Research Institute, 1998), 5, 8.

At the same time, each Eastern Church has its own authentic rite, and the integrity of each rite is properly recognized and upheld by the Catholic Church. As the Second Vatican Council (1962-65) observed, "legitimate diversity is in no way opposed to the Church's unity, but rather emphasizes her splendour and contributes greatly to the fulfilment of her mission."[4] Pope John Paul II returned to this theme in 1995 in *Ut Unum Sint*, as when he asserted, "Full communion is that of unity in legitimate diversity."[5] His title, of course, derives from Jesus' words, "May they all be one" (John 17:21) and is used today to pray for the reunification of the Churches.

In this context, recent actual and proposed changes in liturgical practices and in liturgical texts and music can be best assessed. That is, such changes obviously pertain to the specific Church in which they occur, but at the same time they in truth pertain to the Church as a whole and to reunification. The present study examines several such changes, actual and proposed, in the author's own Metropolia, the Byzantine Catholic Archeparchy of Pittsburgh, which is Ruthenian in origin, deriving from the Eparchy of Mukachiv, in the Transcarpathian Region of western Ukraine, an area evangelized by SS. Cyril and Methodius.[6] Commendably, our Metropolia has been active in the movement toward unity, for instance, through exchanges between the Orthodox and our seminary and through active participation in the annual Orientale Lumen conferences.

Blessed and beautiful restorations are among the recent and proposed changes. It has been prudent and pastoral of our hierarchs to move slowly, even with restorations in practice that are essential to authentic praxis. For even restorations that once again make our practice consonant with those of our sister Churches of the East are changes requiring preparation and time for both clergy and faithful to become familiar with the restoration.

However, a major and wide-sweeping revision is currently under consideration by our hierarchs. Central is the English translation of liturgical texts.[7] On March 25, 2005, when the Feast of the Annunciation coincided with Great and Holy Friday, the Metropolia provided liturgical materials for use on that rare liturgical occasion. This was the first experience that many of the faithful across the Metropolia had with the proposed

---

[4] This point was emphasized by Pope John Paul II in his encyclical, "*Ut unum sint*: The Commitment to Ecumenism" (May 25, 1995), § 50.

[5] *Ut unum sint*, § 54, See also § 57.

[6] For the history of the metropolitanate, see Rt. Rev. Serge Keleher, *The Draft Translation: A Response to the Proposed Recasting of the Byzantine-Ruthenian Divine Liturgy of Saint John Chrysostom*, Studies on the Byzantine Liturgy, 1 (Pittsburgh: Stauropegion Press, 2006), p. 13 et passim.

[7] For a valuable, detailed, and scholarly review of English translations of the Divine Liturgy and of other Eastern liturgical texts, and for excellent bibliography, including reviews of various translations, see Keleher, "Four Translations of the Divine Liturgy." The history of English in Eastern liturgies is extensive (e.g., 267-70, 348ff.) even though the focus is four modern translations.

revisions, both the provisional Divine Liturgy of October 12, 2004, and also the texts and music specific to March 25, 2005. It is excellent that our hierarchy has eschewed undue haste in promulgating the proposed revision, but has instead been receiving the responses of faithful and clergy across the Metropolia and indeed, more broadly.

The following comments are based largely on those liturgical materials used on March 25, 2005. Within the Metropolia, the Eparchy of Van Nuys held a Clergy Day on May 24, 2005, when priests were shown the drafts of the proposed Divine Liturgy, with the instruction that it was not to be copied or given to others. Accordingly, our parish priest allowed me to look through his copy only briefly (for about twenty minutes) and to take notes, and those notes are also reflected in the following pages. I also took a few notes when I experienced a later, somewhat altered version of the revised Divine Liturgy in October 2006 at SS. Cyril and Methodius Byzantine Catholic Seminary in Pittsburgh. The materials were available for use at Divine Liturgy, but not for removal for study.[8]

The comments in the present volume treat three areas:

I. A great joy is the recent restoration of certain authentic elements of Eastern Christian practice, such as praying the Symbol of Faith without the *Filioque*. These restorations are wise implementations of our mission as Eastern Catholics.

II. The goal of attaining more uniform worship throughout the Metropolia is laudable. Principles for translation and revision are clear from historical precedent, including St. Jerome's biblical translation from Greek and Hebrew in the fourth and fifth centuries, and the initial translation for our rite of biblical and liturgical texts from Greek into Slavonic. Sharing the principles evident in these prior projects, the Church's Instruction *Liturgiam Authenticam* (2001) usefully articulates these theological and pastoral principles and is therefore helpful in the present discussion.

III. The changes of March 25, 2005, are of necessity analyzed. Wide-sweeping changes are proposed, in every aspect of text and music. The liturgical use of the venerable Marian title of Theotokos is a splendid advance. Nonetheless, the existence of the traditional Slavonic translation of that title requires further study with regard to when and how the term ought to be rendered in English. The change to "Covenant" in the anaphora looks appropriate, even richly so. Generally, however, the new materials are deficient theologically, musically, and poetically.

Also it appears from dictional changes that our hierarchs intend to show that women are integral to the Church. However, not trendy language but new catechesis and preaching are needed, to articulate for a new-millennial Church the true Catholic

---

[8] On the difficulty of getting access to the proposed new materials, see Keleher, *Response to the Proposed Recasting of the Byzantine-Ruthenian Liturgy*, esp. 47-52 and 267-80.

tradition of respect for the spiritual equality of women existing from the first century.

After the proposed revision had first been used in my parish, SS. Cyril and Methodius Byzantine Catholic Church in Spokane, Washington, on March 25, 2005, I drafted an analysis of it, "The Byzantine Catholic Church in the New Millennium," completed April 28, 2005. Rev. William E. O'Brien, our parish administrator, authorized its posting on the parish's website. The section on "Women and the Church in the New Millennium" I excerpted and expanded; it was accepted for publication in *Saint Vladimir's Theological Quarterly* in June, 2005, [and it appeared there in 2008].[9] It is therefore not reproduced in the present volume. Instead, a concise section on the affirmation of women in the Eastern Catholic Churches has been added, at pages 30-34. Also in the spring of 2005, the editor of a Catholic press requested for publication my full analysis of the proposed revision and allowed me to extend it; the present volume is the result.[10]

Compared to the original analysis of April 28, 2005, several passages in the present work are much revised. This book is more than thrice as long as the original essay. The sections on the Septuagint and on the words "Theotokos," "Holy for the holy," and "Covenant," and the "Excursus on non-liturgical song" with its detailed discussion of Slavonic paraliturgical hymnody are among the new materials. Research on specific liturgical Greek terms was conducted using the Thesaurus Linguae Graecae and other databases at the University of Notre Dame, October 28-29, 2005, and at Dumbarton Oaks in Washington, D.C. This allowed much fuller discussion of the term "Theophilostatos."

Women, language, and worship are recurring issues in this volume of reflections. Language is focal on many levels: the authority of the Greek Old Testament, the role of transliterated Hebrew words in the Greek Old Testament and in Slavonic, the liturgical languages of Greek and Slavonic, and of course both the modern English version of the liturgy in use for decades by 2006 and also the proposed revision of it. Women are prominent because in the new millennium it is fitting and necessary to articulate and affirm more clearly than ever before the salutary Orthodox, Catholic doctrines and practices regarding women. Accomplishing this will require preparation of seminarians in these doctrines and practices, and presentation of them to the faithful. Counter-productive, however, would be politically correct manipulation of Eastern liturgical language, in imitation of the Roman Catholic liturgy in English. Finally, worship is at the heart of the present study, for any proposed change in the liturgy should enable, rather than block, the worship of the faithful. Only a theologically insightful awareness of the breadth of meaning of the full liturgy, words and music, can allow appropriate alteration of the liturgy.

---

[9] [On the use of square brackets in this book, see the third paragraph of the Prologue.]

[10] [The title of this volume was originally "The Byzantine Catholic Church in the New Millennium." Please note that any citations elsewhere to that title are in fact to the present volume.]

4

Chapter 1:

Restorations and Authentic Developments

The past decade has brought to the faithful of our Metropolia, the Byzantine Metropolitan Church *Sui Juris* of Pittsburgh, the joys of returning to important aspects of our authentic Greek Catholic tradition, aspects which had been set aside for a time. Eastern Catholics in the United States had for more than a century accommodated their traditions to those of the Roman Rite, and this was done at least partly out of a laudable desire for unity among all the Catholic faithful. Recently our Holy Pope John Paul II of blessed memory gave sublimely pastoral direction that the Eastern Catholics were to implement again their authentic traditions, most notably administering Holy Communion to newly baptized infants. We owe gratitude to our hierarchs for their pastoral and prudent implementation of such restorations. These enable us to be in our praxis more fully Greek (to speak generally) and Slavic.

Background, Greek and Slavonic

Essential background for appreciating the restorations and authentic developments within the Ruthenian Church involves two linguistic aspects of our heritage. These aspects are also basic to analyzing proposed further changes. Basic to all Greek Christians is the recognition of the foundational importance of the authority of the Septuagint. For the Ruthenian Church, an additional authoritative area is the precedent set by SS. Cyril and Methodius and those who assisted them in translation. In particular, the Slavonic retained certain Hebrew words of worship that the Septuagint had conveyed. In the twenty-first millennium it is still proper to retain those words, transliterating them, rather than translating them.

1. The Authority of the Septuagint

Often Eastern Catholics are diffident about the authority of the Septuagint (called the "Old Greek" in much modern biblical scholarship), even though that is the version of Scripture quoted and referred to in the New Testament.[11] To be authentic to Christian tradition and to maintain our identity with the Orthodox in this regard, it is important

---

[11] [For a detailed discussion of this subject, see also my essay, "Ἀλήθειᾰ Ἑλληνική: The Authority of the Greek Old Testament," completed in August 2010 and now in submission.]

that we affirm and rely upon the validity of the Septuagint.[12] This is important, because the Septuagint and the Greek New Testament are foundational for our liturgy and hymnody, as has been reaffirmed:

> During the 1998 Stamford symposium, Father Archimandrite Robert Taft and other speakers repeatedly stressed that the Hebrew Bible, which almost all the translations of the Psalter use as their basic text, is not the Christian Bible and is not adequate in translating liturgical texts.[13]

In particular, one can cite Psalm 21, famous among Christians because Jesus quoted it upon the Cross. In the Hebrew this psalm certainly seems to have been changed in slight, crucial ways, in reaction to Christianity.[14]

Regrettably, Eastern Catholic Churches in North America, and in some instances Orthodox Churches in North America, now scant the Septuagint. They rely instead on English translations of the biblical text in use by Roman Catholics. That imitation of Roman use constitutes a voluntary Romanization. More properly, this might now be called "Americanization" for it is Roman Catholic praxis in North American specifically that is being privileged.

Biblical scholarship has always properly been multilingual. And Christian biblical scholarship from the apostles through Hippolytus of Rome, Origen, Jerome and other Fathers and on into modernity has often had salutary recourse to Jewish scholarship on the Scriptures, including discussion and analysis of biblical Hebrew.[15] For instance, in his *Commentary on Isaiah*, Jerome reports Jewish commentary on specific passages and compares the textual variants in Hebrew and the more recent Jewish translations into Greek; and Justin Martyr's "astonishingly good knowledge of Judaism" indicates that he

---

[12] Keleher, "Four Translations of the Divine Liturgy" (as in note 2 above) 288, 318, 325, 336, 372, and 392ff.

[13] Keleher, "Four Translations of the Divine Liturgy," 318.

[14] See, e.g., Gilles Dorival, "L'interpretation ancienne du Psaume 21 (22 TM)," in Gilles Dorival, et al., eds., *David, Jesus, et le reine Esther: Recherches sur le Psaume 21(22 TM)*, Collection de la Revue des Études Juives 25 (Paris: Peeters, 2002), 225-314, here at p. 293; and Michaela Burks, "Le Psaume 21 (22 TM) dans le recherche veterotestamentaire du XXe siècle," in ibid., 341-92, here 347-48. See also Tkacz, "Esther, Jesus and Psalm 22," pp. 724-25.

[15] For instance, Hippolytus of Rome (ca. 200), *Commentary on Daniel* 1.14 (SC 14: 1947), p. 96; Origen, *Epistula ad Africanum*, pars. 6, 12 (PG 11:61, 76-78); Origen, *Stromateis 10* (PG 11:101, 104); Jerome, *In Hieremiam prophetam* 5.67 (CCL 74:283-85). See also Benjamin Kedar-Kopfstein, *The Vulgate as a Translation: Some Semantic and Syntactical Aspects of Jerome's Version of the Hebrew Bible* (Ph.D. diss.: University of Jerusalem, 1968); Jay Braverman, *Jerome's Commentary on Daniel: A Study of Comparative Jewish and Christian Interpretations of the Hebrew Bible* (Washington, D.C.: Catholic Biblical Association of America, 1978); Adam Kamesar, *Jerome, Greek Scholarship and the Hebrew Bible: A Study of the "Quaestiones Hebraicae in Genesim,"* Oxford Classical Monograph (Oxford: Clarendon Press, 1993).

"was in a kind of academic dialogue with the large Jewish community in Rome."[16] The Syriac Fathers likewise drew deeply on Jewish interpretation of the Book of Daniel.[17] This engagement with Jewish scriptural studies is part of a larger Jewish-Christian interaction, sometimes involving debates.[18] Origen and Jerome recorded and transmitted Jewish commentary on the Hebrew Bible to the West. In many instances, the only way in which this Jewish commentary was preserved was in the writings of Christians.

What is often neglected today, however, is that the Jewish version of Scriptures that was well known in Jerusalem in the first century and that resonates in the Greek New Testament was not Hebrew, but Greek. (Complicating the situation is that no pre-Christian manuscripts survive of either the Hebrew version of the Old Testament or of the Septuagint.) The Gospels, the Acts of the Apostles, the Epistles and the Apocalypse quote, paraphrase, and allude to the scriptures as they existed in Greek, the pre-Christian Jewish translations into Greek of what is for Christians the Old Testament.

This point received salutary public commendation when our Holy Pontiff Benedict XVI spoke eloquently of the Greek Old Testament at Regensburg on September 20, 2006:

> Today we know that the Greek translation of the Old Testament produced at Alexandria – the Septuagint – is more than a simple (and in that sense perhaps less than satisfactory) translation of the Hebrew text: it is an independent textual witness and a distinct and important step in the history of revelation, one which

---

[16] Jerome, *Commentarii in Isaiam prophetam,* passim (PL 24:76, 87); on Justin: Martin Hengel, *The Septuagint as Christian Scripture: Its Prehistory and the Problem of its Canon,* 2nd ed. (Grand Rapids: Baker Academic, 2004), 34.

[17] As documented by Maurice Casey, *Son of Man: The Interpretation of Daniel 7* (London: SPCK, 1979), chapter 3. His account shows a curiously patronizing attitude toward the Syriac Fathers, however: He attributes all use of the Gospels in Syriac discussions of Daniel to an oppressive Western influence upon the East, although it is far more likely that the Syriac Fathers, being Christians, simply read the Gospels and recognized the quotations from the book of Daniel.

[18] Lawrence Lahey, "Jewish Biblical Interpretation and the Genuine Jewish-Christian Debate in The Dialogue of Timothy and Aquila," *Journal of Jewish Studies* 51.2 (2000): 281-96; idem, "Hebrew and Aramaic in the *Dialogue of Timothy and Aquila,*" in *Hebrew Study from Ezra to Ben-Yehuda,* ed. William Harbury (Edinburgh: T & T Clark, 1999), pp. 106-21; and idem, "The Christian-Jewish Dialogues through the Sixth Century (excluding Justin)" in *A History of Jewish Believers in Jesus: The First Five Centuries,* ed. Oskar Skarsaune and Reidar Hvalvik, = A History of Jewish Believers in Jesus from Antiquity to the Present, vol. 1 (Peabody, MS: Hendrickson Publishers, in press (cited from typescript). Some of these debates were recorded in transcripts. One such record is the basis of *The Dialogue of Gregentius Archbishop of Taphar with Herban a Jew:* Lahey, "Christian-Jewish Dialogues," pp. 27-34. In this text, the speeches of the Jewish participant "often are at least a paragraph, and in numerous places are longer than those of Gregentius; there is also lengthy back and forth discussion on individual issues. These are what one would expect from a genuine debate"; ibid., p. 32. See also A. B. Hulen, "The 'Dialogues with the Jews' as Sources for the Early Jewish Argument against Christianity," *Journal of Biblical Studies* 51 (1932): 58-70.

brought about this encounter in a way that was decisive for the birth and spread of Christianity. A profound encounter of faith and reason is taking place here, an encounter between genuine enlightenment and religion.

...The New Testament was written in Greek and bears the imprint of the Greek spirit, which had already come to maturity as the Old Testament developed.[19]

As the pope affirmed, for Christians the authoritative Old Testament is the pre-Christian Greek. This pre-Christian Greek consists mainly of the Old Greek (Septuagint) but also includes so-called Theodotion-Daniel. In the first century before Christ, Palestinian Jewish scholars, working from superior manuscripts, no longer extant, corrected problems with the Old Greek version of the Book of Daniel and prepared a new Greek translation of that book with all fourteen chapters. It is now referred to as "Theodotion-Daniel," because a century or so later Theodotion incorporated that version of Daniel into his full translation of the Old Testament. Analogously, St. Jerome would later incorporate Old Latin translations of Wisdom, Sirach, Baruch, and 1-4 Maccabees without revision into the Vulgate.[20] Significantly, it is Theodotion-Daniel and not Septuagint-Daniel that is quoted in the New Testament.[21] Not surprisingly, Theodotion-Daniel also underlies certain passages in the Divine Liturgy, such as the precommunion confession, "One is holy" (Dan. 8:13), cited in the Apostolic Constitutions VII, 35:3.[22] For the prophet-book of Daniel, the version adopted by Theodotion was authoritative for pre-Christian Jews and accordingly for the early Christians. Indeed, in the modern critical edition of the Septuagint by Alfred Rahlfs, that scholar includes both the Septuagint text for the Book of Daniel and also Theodotion-Daniel. One also finds a few recent scholars likewise giving scholarly

---

[19] The full text is available online: http://www.vatican. va/holy_father/ benedict_xvi/speeches/2006/september/documents/hf_ben-xvi_spe_200609 12_university-regensburg_en.html.

[20] Catherine Brown Tkacz, "*Labor tam utilis*: The Creation of the Vulgate," *Vigiliae Christianae* 50.1 (1996): 42-72., at 51-52; *Biblia Sacra iuxta vulgatam versionem*, ed. Robert Weber, with the assistance of B. Fischer, J. Gribomont, H. F. D. Sparks, and W. Thiele; 4ᵃ rev. ed. prepared by Roger Gryson with B. Fischer, H. I. Frede, H. F. D. Sparks, and W. Thiele (Stuttgart: Deutsche Bibelgesellschaft, 1994), vol. 1, p. xx.

[21] See, e.g., Hengel, *Septuagint as Christian Scripture*, 113; Anthony A. Di Lella, O.F.M., in *The Book of Daniel: A New Translation with Notes and Commentary on Chapters 1-9 by † Louis F. Hartman, C.SS.R.; Introduction and Commentary on Chapters 10-12 by Alexander A. Di Lella, O.F.M.*, Anchor Bible (Garden City, N.Y.: Doubleday & Company, Inc., 1978), 81, 82; and Charles J. Obiajunwa, "Semitic Interference in Theodotion-Daniel" (Ph.D. diss.: The Catholic University of America 1999), 6-7.

[22] Robert F. Taft, "'Holy Things for the Saints': The Ancient Call to Communion and Its Response," in *Fountain of Life: In Memory of Niels K. Rasmussen, O.P.*, ed. Gerard Austin (Washington, D.C.: Pastoral Press, 1991), 87-102, at pp. 93-94.

emphasis to the value of the Greek Old Testament, in particular, the Book of Daniel.[23]

Regarding women, one may note that the Greek Old Testament contains distinctive features that are decidedly favorable to women. This is a new point, and it has not been stated in print before. The authoritative nature of the Septuagint and Theodotion-Daniel are the primary reason for Eastern Catholics to respect that version of Scripture. In addition, however, the positive presentation of women in that version definitely indicates another reason for respecting and relying upon the Greek Old Testament. Two main instances in which the Greek Old Testament favors women have been documented to date. The Greek Old Testament placed Susanna at the head of the book of Daniel. Thus her example of heroically risking her life in order to uphold her faith prepares for the heroism of the Three Youths and of Daniel himself. Indeed, she gave them the example to follow in their own ordeals. Jephthah's daughter likewise has an importance in Christian tradition which is enhanced by the Septuagint's distinctive description (not shared by the Masoretic Text). In the Septuagint both she and Isaac are described as "only begotten" and as "beloved" (ἀγαπητος / ἀγαπητή).[24] This Greek diction resonates in Gospel passages including the synoptic accounts of the Baptism and Transfiguration.[25] As a result of this inspired Greek parallel between the Jephthah's daughter and Isaac, Eastern tradition has a stronger basis for interpreting this daughter as well as this son as types of Christ, the beloved Son of the Father. For a woman to be a type of Christ points powerfully to the equal capacity of the sexes to become holy, as discussed below. The Septuagint and Theodotion-Daniel contribute to this typology.

Several cogent reasons, then, indicate that the authority of the pre-Christian Jewish translation of the Old Testament into Greek ought to be honored. Certainly Greek Catholics especially ought to respect the authority of the Greek Scriptures.

The pre-Christian Jewish translators of the Septuagint revered and retained certain holy words in Hebrew, merely transliterating the sounds into Greek characters so

---

[23] "Theodotion-Daniel," in *The Book of Daniel: Composition and Reception*, ed. John J. "Collins and Peter W. Flint with the assistance of Cameron Van Epps, 2 vols. (Leiden: Brill, 2002, vol. 2, pp. 586-607, at 595-96, 604-05, refining his prior statement: Di Lella, *Book of Daniel*, pp. 81-82. See also Catherine Brown Tkacz, "ἀνεβόησεν φωνῇ μεγάλῃ: Susanna and the Synoptic Passion Narratives," *Gregorianum* 87.3 (2006) 449-86. Also, there is a critical edition of this book: *Susanna, Daniel, Bel et Draco*, ed. J. Ziegler and O. Munnich, Septuaginta: Vetus Testamentum Graecum 16,2; 2d ed. (Göttingen: Vandendhoeck & Ruprecht, 1999).

[24] Albert J. Paretsky, O.P., *Jewish Eschatological Expectation and the Transfiguration of Christ* (Rome, 1985): "The Beloved," 88-90.

[25] Diction from Judges 11 appears to nuance "the synoptic accounts of the Baptism (Matt. 3:17, Mark 1:11, Luke 3:22, 2 Pet 1:17) and Transfiguration (Matt. 17:5, Mark 9:7; Luke 9:35…), Matthew's quotation of Isaiah 42:1-4 (Matt. 12:17-21), and the parable of the vineyard (Mark 12:6, Luke 20:13), as well as the Johannine declaration of John 3:16": Catherine Brown Tkacz, "Women as Types of Christ: Susanna and Jephthah's Daughter," *Gregorianum* 85.2 (2004): 281-314, quotation from 296.

that the faithful could pronounce them. These particularly holy Hebrew words include *Pascha, alleluia, hosanna, sabaoth, cherubim,* and *seraphim.*[26] For instance, the Septuagint in reporting Isaiah's vision of the angels adoring God retains the Hebrew word naming the Lord, simply transliterating it into Greek as Σαβαώθ (*Sabaoth*).[27] Greek Christians continued this Jewish practice, evidently wanting to worship in words expressive of the original divine revelation to the Jews. In the West, however, in the Vulgate Jerome retained only some of these words. He kept *Alleluia,* which appears as the heading of Psalm 118, but he translated other terms into Latin. Thus in Psalm 118:25 he translated *hosanna* as *salvum fac* ("save [me]"). Likewise, in Isaiah's account of his vision of the angelic praises of God (Isa. 6:3) Jerome rendered *sabaoth* as *Dominus exercituum* ("Lord of hosts / armies").[28] Evincing in this regard more respect for the authority of the pre-Christian Greek Scriptures, the Eastern churches kept all these words, merely transliterating them into Greek.

The word "Amen / *Amin*" is a special case. Although the Greek Old Testament lacks it, Jesus used it. Thus it is found in both the New Testament and the Divine Liturgy, in both Greek and Slavonic.[29]

2. *Slavonic precedent in biblical translations and transliteration*

The Slavonic tradition is likewise faithful to the Greek precedent in retaining these Hebrew terms and merely transliterating them into Slavonic. The word found in Isaiah's vision of angelic praise, rendered in Greek characters as Σαβαώθ in the Septuagint, was accordingly transliterated into Slavonic for the Divine Liturgy. It would be best for modern English translations of the Slavonic also to retain the heavenly word *Sabaoth*. In contrast, it would be Latinizing / Americanizing to copy from the International Commission on English in the Liturgy (ICEL) by substituting for Sabaoth the formulation, "Lord, God of power and might," which is not even a translation of the Hebrew.[30]

---

[26] The last three of these terms are discussed below in their occurrence in the Slavonic hymn *Vs'i T'a Chory.*

[27] Isaias 6:3: Keleher, "Four Translations of the Divine Liturgy" (as in note 2 above), 336.

[28] For Jerome's discussions of some important Hebrew words including the Jewish names for God and the terms "Alleluia," "Amen," "Maranatha," "Selah," "ephod," and "teraphim," see his Letters 25-26, 28-29.

[29] Jerome's Vulgate has "Amen" only in the Psalms from the Hebrew and in the New Testament, and elsewhere in the Old Testament it translates it as *fiat,* "so be it," in parallel to the Septuagint's translation γένοιτο. For pertinent scriptures, see Matt. 6:13 (last word of the Our Father), Rom. 16:27 (last word of the epistle), Apoc. 3:14; Num. 5:22, Deut. 27:15-26, Pss. 40:14 (41:13), 71:19 (72:19), 88:53 (89:5) and 105:48 (106:48).

[30] For the route by which ICEL's formulation entered some English translations of the Divine Liturgy, see Keleher, "Four Translations of the Divine Liturgy," 336-37.

Other Greek terms, however, are different. Terms such as Τριάδα (in Roman letters: *Triada*) and Θεοτόκος (*Theotokos*) are not from the Septuagint but were coined by Christians in the first centuries of Christianity to express new revelations and doctrines. SS. Cyril and Methodius and their followers treated these words differently from the ancient Hebrew words that had been transliterated into Greek. These new Christian words were not transliterated, but were actually translated into Slavonic, as *Trojce* and *Bohoróditsa*. This diction is also part of the authentic Slavonic liturgical tradition. English also translates the terms, rendering *Trojce* as "Trinity." Θεοτόκος / *Bohoróditsa* is a critically important and special case, to be discussed below.

Still much needed is fuller study of the Greek scriptures *per se*, an appropriate translation into English of them,[31] and analysis of how the Slavonic liturgy handles the Greek, including which terms it transliterates and which ones it translates, and how. These are among the prerequisites for definitive consideration of any English translation of the liturgy and its hymn-texts. It ought not to be the case that, in translating the Slavonic liturgy into English, the Slavonic "washes out" as if it were irrelevant and the Greek alone is respected. Both must be honored, if the integrity of the rite is to be maintained.

Restorations and Authentic Developments

With that said, we turn to some specific restorations and authentic developments of the decade centered on the turn of the century, 1996-2005. Prior to that had occurred the important recovery of the restoration of the Liturgy of the Presanctified Gifts, as Archimandrite Father Keleher has noted.[32] In the decade in question our Metropolia has brought about certain restorations in practice of what has always been Greek Catholic tradition. These restorations implement the call of Vatican II for the Eastern Churches to restore authentic aspects of their traditions.

1. Filioque

The return to the Nicene Creed's original sense, without the *Filioque*, is a case in point. In 1990, Bishop Andrew Pataki of the Eparchy of Parma, Ohio, directed that the *Filioque* ("and the Son") not be added to the Creed during Divine Liturgies within his eparchy. On June 29, 1995, Pope John Paul II, in the presence of the Ecumenical Patriarch Bartholomew I, urged that there be clarification of the full harmony between the liturgical Latin Credo's *Filioque* and the creed of the Ecumenical Council of Constantinople in 381. This clarification followed within weeks when the Pontifical

---

[31] For existing English translations of the Septuagint Psalter, see Keleher, "Four Translations of the Divine Liturgy," *passim*.

[32] Keleher, *Response to the Proposed Recasting of the Byzantine-Ruthenian Liturgy* (as in note 6 above), pp. 5-6.

Council for Promoting Christian Unity published "The Procession of the Holy Spirit: The Greek and Latin Traditions" in September.[33] Now throughout the Metropolia the Symbol of Faith is prayed without the *Filioque*.

2. *Infant communication*

The Metropolia has also restored the authentic Eastern practice of communicating the Eucharist to newly baptized infants. In an accommodation to Roman practice, many parishes had withheld the Eucharist from baptized and chrismated infants and children and had observed a "first communion" for children of the age of reason, in imitation of Latin procedure. As Father Archimandrite Robert F. Taft, S.J., has noted, the Western setting aside of infant communion was a medieval development, not authentic early practice, so it is entirely fitting that the Eastern rites resume their normal practice.[34] Now, once again, throughout our Metropolia newly baptized babies are chrismated and then receive the Holy Eucharist. This is an important restoration. The Catechism of the Catholic Church praises this practice:

> First Holy Communion. Having become a child of God clothed with the wedding garment, the neophyte is admitted "to the marriage supper of the Lamb" and receives the food of the new life, the body and blood of Christ. The Eastern Churches maintain a lively awareness of the unity of Christian initiation by giving Holy Communion to all the newly baptized and confirmed, even little children, recalling the Lord's words, "Let the children come to me, do not hinder them."[35]

3. *Postures of worship*

The return to the Byzantine posture of standing or sitting, not kneeling, during Pascha has also been most welcome. The postures and gestures of worship by the faithful remain an area for formation: The cherubic posture – standing, with arms crossed on the breast, like a cherub with two of its six wings folded – is never used by many of the faithful. The renewed practice of not kneeling during Pascha gives physical expression to

---

[33] "The *Filioque*: Healing an Ancient Source of Division between the Catholic and Orthodox Churches," *Catholic International* 7.1 (January 1996): 36-49. See also Keleher, "Four Translations of the Divine Liturgy," 282-283; and Archimandrite Boniface (Luykx), "Thirty Years Later: Reflections on Vatican II's *Unitatis Redintegratio* and *Orientalium Ecclesiarum*," *Logos* 34 (1993): 364-387, at 385.

[34] Archimandrite Robert F. Taft, S.J., "The Liturgy in the Life of the Church," *Logos: A Journal of Eastern Christian Studies* 40.1-4 (1999), 203: Keleher, *Response to the Proposed Recasting of the Byzantine-Ruthenian Liturgy*, 45.

[35] *Catechism of the Catholic Church*, 2d ed., revised in accordance with the official Latin text promulgated by Pope John Paul II (Libreria Editrice Vaticana, English translation 1997, Glossary and *Index Analyticus*, 2000), '1244, quoting Apoc. 19:9 and Mark 10:14. See also §1233.

the contrast between the Great Fast with its suppliant and contrite prostrations and Pascha with its return to standing upright in the presence of the Lord, a posture which is emblematic of the ongoing sanctification of the individual.

4. *"To You, O Lord."*

Another wisely chosen, pastoral restoration of liturgical practice is of a different nature: It concerns pruning an elaboration that had developed within the Slavic rite. The elaboration involved the congregation's singing of "To You, O Lord," after the "Our Father" and in response to the celebrant's direction, "Bow your heads to the Lord." The music for "To You, O Lord," had become elaborated and the words were sung twice, so that they in fact covered most of the celebrant's prayer. As Basil Shereghy observed: "This prayer can be considered an official pleading for God's special blessing before Holy Communion. It can be found as early as the Anaphora of St. Hippolytus (third cent.) and in the Liturgy of the Apostolic Constitutions."[36] The return ca. 2004 to singing the phrase "To You, O Lord," just once and to a shorter musical setting allows the faithful to hear the celebrant's words in the prayer. For this change, slight as it may seem, our hierarchs deserve the praise of the faithful, because the change recognizes the active participation of the faithful as we prayerfully, silently affirm what the celebrant is voicing.[37]

5. *Our Lady of Guadelupe*

Another laudable change is an authentic development rather than a restoration. Once Pope John Paul II had, in 1999, declared December 12 a Liturgical holy day for the whole of North America, our church needed new hymnody for this feast. The most fitting Troparion and Kontakion of Our Lady of Guadelupe, provided to the parishes on Sunday, December 12, 2001, are a wonderful addition to the hymnody of the Slavic rite, an addition for which we are indebted to Bishop Andrew Pataki and Fr. David Petras and signally to the monastic hymnode.[38] Moreover, it is profoundly pastoral that Hispanic people have the joy of the whole church singing praises of the Theotokos' appearance in the New World and her ἀχειροπόητα icon (*acheiropoeta*, "made without human hand").

---

[36] Basil Shereghy, *The Divine Liturgy of Saint John Chrysostom* (Pittsburgh: Byzantine Seminary Press, 1970), pp. 214-215.

[37] This pastoral respect for the faithful is identical to that evident in *"Liturgiam Authenticam*: On the use of Vernacular Languages in the Publication of the Books of the Roman Liturgy," Fifth Instruction "For the Right Implementation of the Constitution on the Sacred Liturgy of the Second Vatican Council (*Sacrosanctum Concilium*, art. 36), by the Congregation for Divine Worship and the Discipline of the Sacraments, issued 28 March 2001, § 64, discussed below at pages 37-38.

[38] Bishop Andrew approved the texts, and Fr. David Petras is identified in the credits as the one who published the text in the "proposed liturgical texts of the Inter-Eparchial Liturgy Commission" in the 2001 Typikon. This information, including the texts quoted, is taken from the music leaflets copyrighted by John Vernoski in 2001. The hymnode, I think, was a monk of Holy Resurrection Monastery.

Including in the Troparion Juan Diego's name and the correct term for the miraculously affected garment, his tilma, is perfect, as is clarifying its nature in the phrase "cactus cloth" in the Kontakion. The eloquence of these verses is, moreover, characteristically Eastern: Repeating a word with different nuances is a poetic trait of Eastern hymnody that encourages contemplation. For instance, one finds: "Give a word (*slovo*) to me, O Word (*Slovo*) of the Father."[39] The Troparion for Our Lady of Guadelupe has meaningful word play in the words "sun" and "Son" and also has clear, unemotionalized reference to blood, expressed in graceful English: "No longer shall the New World lie wounded in useless blood sacrifice, for she who is clothed with the sun has revealed the Son to us."

The prayerful analogy of the next two lines is likewise quite Eastern in tone, for it prompts reverence and contemplation of mystery: "O Mother of the Americas, imprint his name upon our hearts, just as you wove your image upon the cactus cloth." The conclusion of the Kontakion rightly builds to the people's directly addressing God: "Teach your children to cry out: 'O Christ our God, our hope, glory to you.'" Finally, these proper hymns were clearly set to our chant tones (Tones 4 and 7) and therefore these hymns were immediately singable, which means, for Eastern Catholics, immediately available to the faithful as their prayer.

[Unfortunately, this new feast is absent from the revised *Divine Liturgy*.[40]]

6. *Theotokos*

On March 25, 2005, the splendid term "Theotokos" appeared in the liturgies of our Metropolia.[41] This liturgical use of the "canonized dogmatic term Theotokos" is

---

[39] *The Divine Liturgy: A Book of Prayer for the Liturgies of St. John Chrysostom and St. Basil the Great* B hereafter, *Divine Liturgy* (1978) B designed, compiled and adapted by Rev. William Levkulic (Pittsburgh: Byzantine Seminary Press, 1978), 76.

[40] [This feast should have appeared in the revised *Divine Liturgy* after p. 280. On the use of square brackets in this book, see the third paragraph of the Prologue.]

[41] For instance, pp. 9, 41 and the title page of *The Divine Liturgy of Our Holy Father John Chrysostom with Vespers for Holy and Great Friday and The Feast of the Annunciation of the Theotokos and Ever-Virgin Mary: When Holy and Great Friday is on MARCH 25*, Priest/Cantor edition. "At the direction of the Council of Hierarchs of the Byzantine Metropolitan Church Sui Juris of Pittsburgh, U.S.A., the text of this booklet has been prepared by the Metropolitan Liturgical Commission and the music by the Metropolitan Music Commission. It is the official text for use when Great and Holy Friday falls on March 25, the feast of the Annunciation, on which day Vespers with the Divine Liturgy of St. John Chrysostom is to be celebrated no earlier than 3:00 p.m. This text and music has been approved by the Council of Hierarchs and promulgated by Metropolitan Basil Schott in accordance with the Sacred Canons. No other text is to be used on this occasion in the churches of the Byzantine Metropolitan Church *Sui Juris* of Pittsburgh, U.S.A. Nihil obstat: The Very Rev. Archpriest David M. Petras, S.E.O.D.. Imprimatur: +The Most Rev. Basil M. Schott, O.F.M., D.D., Metropolitan Archbishop of Pittsburgh, February 16, 2005." In the following notes this material will be cited to as "2005 Great Friday

hailed as a "notable improvement" by Archimandrite Serge Keleher in his recent, insightful monograph.[42] For the Slavonic tradition of worship, use of the word Theotokos is not a restoration per se.[43] It nonetheless represents, as will be seen, a wonderful recovery of theologically and culturally rich worship. How beautifully our hierarchs timed its introduction at Liturgy to occur on the Feast of the Annunciation, for the word Theotokos is a profoundly incarnational title for Mary.[44]

Nonetheless, as discussed below, the English version of the Divine Liturgy already in use for decades had rendered *Bohoróditsa* in Western fashion, as "Mother of God." Therefore, the parishes of the Metropolia were unprepared for the term Theotokos. This was particularly the case in those parishes which do not sing Marian hymns with the word *Bohoróditsa* or its free English translation "God-bearer." (For the ambiguity of "Godbearer," however, see below.)

This pastoral point, namely that the people were unprepared for use of the word "Theotokos," might have been foreseen by the committees producing the revised Liturgy, and accordingly they might have advised the hierarchs that the introduction of the term Theotokos warranted special care. In 1996 the Eastern Catholic Churches received from the Oriental Congregation a reminder of the importance of "careful [pastoral] investigation" before the revision of any part of the Liturgy occurs.[45] Their reminder is in fact in the form of a quotation from the Vatican II document, *Sacrosanctum Concilium.*[46] For the Pittsburgh Metropolitinate, introduction of the word "Theotokos" constitutes a revision of more than a single part of the Liturgy: This single change affects nearly every part of the Liturgy, and accordingly the change should all the more have been a matter for pastoral concern and preparation.

Probably it could have best been handled in the way that the restoration of infant communication had been, as a solitary change, prepared for carefully and over several months, and only then instituted. Even then, although the transliterated form Theotokos

Vespers." The term "Theotokos" also appears in the *Supplement for Strasti Matins For Holy and Great Friday and The Feast of the Annunciation of the Theotokos and Ever-Virgin Mary, 25 March 2005.*

[42] Keleher, *Response to the Proposed Recasting of the Byzantine-Ruthenian Liturgy* (as in note 6 above), p. 131.

[43] In my initial comments in April 2005 on the proposed changes in the Divine Liturgy, I mistakenly characterized the use of the word *Theotokos* as a restoration.

[44] For this title as calling attention to the Incarnation, see Catherine Brown Tkacz, "Reproductive Science and the Incarnation," *Fellowship of Catholic Scholars Quarterly* 25.4 (Fall, 2002): 11-25.

[45] Oriental Congregation, *Instruction for Applying the Liturgical Prescriptions of the Code of Canons of the Eastern Churches* (Vatican City: Libreria Editrice Vaticana, 1996), citing Constitution of the Sacred Liturgy, n. 23: Keleher, *Response to the Proposed Recasting of the Byzantine-Ruthenian Liturgy*, pp. 9798, 107.

[46] *Sacrosanctum Concilium*, 1964: http://www.vatican.va/archive/hist_councils/ii_vatican_council/documents/vat-ii_const_19631204_sacrosa nctum-concilium_en.html

15

is probably the best term to use in the Divine Liturgy, it most probably should not completely replace *Bohoróditsa* or English equivalents in preaching and hymnody. For the word *Bohoróditsa* is an inspired and venerable translation of the word Theotokos.

a. "Theotokos" and "Mater theou." The very word Θεοτόκος is mysterious, a profound expression of the reality of the Incarnation. The word is prominent in the Divine Liturgy and in several of the Marian proper hymns throughout the year. In Christian use by at least the third century, it is known from a troparion and from the writings of Hippolytus of Rome.[47] East and West were united in upholding the term, for when Cyril of Alexandria defended this title, he was endorsed by a Roman Synod under Pope Celestine I and also by the Council of Ephesus (431).[48] In the tradition derived from SS. Cyril and Methodius, the term Θεοτόκος was consistently represented in the Divine Liturgy and in Marian hymns by the word *Bohoróditsa*, which appears to be a skillful and reverent rendering of the venerable Greek title for Mary into Slavic. In Greek and in Slavonic, this title for Mary is unique, created specifically for Mary. Θεοτόκος / *Bohoróditsa* is found in the Divine Liturgy in the first Ektene (ectenia, litany), in the refrain to the usual antiphons, in the Hymn of the Incarnation, and in a further Ektene.[49] The focal term also occurs in the irmoi for the Entrance into the Temple and for the Conception of Anne, and in the troparia, kontakia, and irmoi for the Annunciation and the Dormition.[50]

"Mother of God" is a distinct and separate designation in both Greek and Slavonic: Μήτηρ Θεοῦ in Greek, well known through inscriptions on icons; and *Bohomati* in Slavonic. This designation for Mary is found in the final prayer of the Divine Liturgy and in the Troparion for October 1.[51] The Greek phrase Μήτηρ Θεοῦ may be a deliberate variation of Elizabeth's designation of Mary as μήτηρ τοῦ κυρίου μου ("mother of my Lord"), using the explicit Θεοῦ, "God," to make overt what is already evident in κυρίου, "Lord." The word κύριος was often used as a "designation of Israel's God" in the

---

[47] Hugo Rahner, in *Zeitschrift für Katholische Theologie* 59 (1935): 73-81, cited by Podskalsky (see next note).

[48] Gerhard Podskalsky, "Theotokos," in *The Oxford Dictionary of Byzantium* [hereafter *ODB*], 3 vols., ed. Alexander P. Kazhdan (Oxford, 1991), s.v. See also John A. Hardon, S.J., *The Catholic Catechism: A Contemporary Catechism of the Teachings of the Catholic Church* (Garden City: Doubleday & Company, 1975), 133-138.

[49] The word Θεοτόκος recurs several times in the *Divine Liturgy*. See, for instance, Η ΘΕΙΑ ΛΕΙΤΟΥΡΓΙΑ ΤΟΥ ΕΝ ΑΓΙΟΙΣ ΠΑΤΡΟΣ ΗΜΩΝ ΙΩΑΝΝΟΥ ΤΟΥ ΧΡΥΣΟΣΤΟΜΟΥ (Rome, 1950), 24, 25, 26, 27, 30, 44, 52, 66. This volume is viewable online: http://www.patronagechurch. com/Liturgikon%20E&S/The%20Liturgikon.htm. Bohoróditsa: See *Divine Liturgy* (1978), 7, 8, 10, 27.

[50] Богородица: ЦЕРКОВНОЕ ПРОСТОПѢНІЕ, I. Gorman (1906), No. 34 (pp. 98-100), 36 (pp. 106-08), 38 (pp. 110-11), 40 (pp. 113-15). For these, transliterated into Roman characters: *Divine Liturgy* (1978), 103, 105, 12829, 140-41.

[51] *ΘΕΙΑ ΛΕΙΤΟΥΡΓΙΑ* (1950), pp. 61, 68: ἀειπαρθένου Μητρός ("ever-virgin Mother") and Μητρός. *Bohomati*: See *Divine Liturgy* (1978), 28 and 97. See also pp. 105-106.

Septuagint, replacing the Tetragrammaton (YHWH) of the Hebrew.[52] Thus Elizabeth's recognition of Mary as "Mother of my Lord" is a profoundly Jewish response to the Incarnation. That is, Elizabeth's words acknowledge the unborn child as God, and she does so in a characteristically Jewish manner, by using the word "Lord" to indicate God.

The Latin Church rendered *Theotokos* in three ways: with a new Latin title, *Deipara*; less directly, as *Dei Genetrix*; and, least directly, as *Mater Dei*.[53] The arresting distinctiveness of the Greek word (discussed below) is clearly what caused it to have three Latin translations: *Deipara*, which is likewise unique and distinctive; *Dei genetrix*, which is close in etymology but which has moved toward familiar language; and *Mater Dei*, which is a readily understandable, simple form of the title. The phrase *Dei Genetrix* is offered as a Latin rendering of Theotokos by Arnobius Junior, Cassiodorus, and the Venerable Bede, for instance, who call attention to how the term Theotokos emphasizes the mystery of the Incarnation.[54]

b. *Bohoróditsa* conflated with *Bohomati*. Unfortunately, when English versions of the Slavonic liturgy began to be used, it appears that *Bohoróditsa* was conflated with *Bohomati*. The two different terms were translated as if they were identical. Both were rendered "Mother of God," which is the meaning of *Bohomati*.[55] Ironically, the far more frequently used term *Bohoróditsa*, the Slavonic rendering of Theotokos, the conciliar title for Mary, had no distinctive presence in the English version of the liturgy. It would have been more authentic to the tradition if in the English the word had reverted to the original Greek, Theotokos, or had been retained as distinctively Slavonic, *Bohoróditsa*, or had been translated into English. The easier course, though, was to simplify the language and use "Mother of God." This omission from worship in English of an important term can lead to simplification and misrepresentation of doctrine.[56] Further, it appears that the

---

[52] Robert Hanhart, "Problems in the History of the LXX Text from Its Beginnings to Origen," the Introduction to Hengel, *Septuagint as Christian Scripture* (as in note 15 above), 1-17, at 7-8.

[53] An instance of "mater domini" being used to translate *Theotokos* is found in Arnobius Junior, *Conflictus cum Serapione*, 2.14.760. Usually he translates the Greek as "Dei genetrix": see next note. Notably, the primary Latin term created to render "Theotokos" in English is *Deipara*, a word comparable to Θεοτόκος, because the word *Deipara* was invented as a Latin counterpart to Θεοτόκος, and, like that word, also derives from the words for "God" (*Deus*) and "to give birth" (*pario*).

[54] Arnobius Junior, *Conflictus cum Serapione* 2.8, line 347; see also lines 307, 350, and 2.10.467, et passim, and his *Praedestinatus* 89, page 54, line 5; Cassiodorus, *Expositio psalmorum*, on Psalm 58 (CCL 97:line 36); Bede, *In Lucae evangelium expositio* 1.1.596. Arnobius in particular writes of Mary's role in the Incarnation *in utero* and *in partu*: 2.15.821. See also Peter Chrysologus, *Sermo 145* (CCL 24B, line 76), and the monk Scytha, *Disputatio*, 4a:49. The database Library of Latin Texts from Brepols, used at Dumbarton Oaks in Washington, D.C., was invaluable for this aspect of the research.

[55] For details, see Keleher, "Four Translations of the Divine Liturgy" (as in note 2 above), 305. See also *Divine Liturgy* (1978), 7, 8, 10, and 27 and, for Marian troparia, kontakia, and irmoi in which *Bohoróditsa* is rendered "Mother of God," 103, 105-106.

[56] See below at pp. 38-39, for instance.

preference for "Mother of God" is a Western influence. In short, the exclusive use in the liturgy of the designation "Mother of God" without use of *Bohoróditsa* or a true English equivalent, was a Romanization. To see this requires looking at the history of the important term, Θεοτόκος.

c. Etymology of the term "Theotokos." The word "Theotokos" in its very construction acknowledges and honors the Incarnation as a real historical event, prophesied by Isaiah, announced by Gabriel to Mary, angelically announced to Joseph and to the shepherds, and recounted in the Gospels. In each case, the biblical language is unequivocal in foretelling and then reporting a real physical conception and birth. Consistently in all the pertinent passages in Scripture the same verb is found, namely the verb "to give birth" (τίκτω, in Roman letters *tikto*). That word is related etymologically to the noun *tokos* which forms the second half of the word Theotokos.

The lexical origins of the word "Theotokos" are clearly the Septuagint and the Gospels. Isaiah foretold that a virgin would ἐν γαστρί ἕξει καὶ τέξεται ὁ υἱόν ("conceive in her womb and bear [i.e., give birth to, τέξεται] a son"; 7:14). The prophecy was explicit in foretelling a human conception and birth, thus ruling out the possibility that a virgin foster mother could suffice to fulfill the prophecy. Moreover, Gabriel's annunciatory words are quite close to Isaiah's prophecy, mainly changed to personalize them to Mary in the second-person singular: συλλήμψη ἐν γαστρί καὶ τέξῃ υἱόν ("you shall conceive in [your] womb and bear [i.e., give birth to, τέξῃ] a son" Luke 1:31). The unambiguous word τίκτω, indicating biological reproduction, is also recorded in Luke's narration of Jesus' birth (ἔτεκεν τον υἱόν , Luke 2:7) and in the angels' annunciation to the shepherds (ἐτέχθη, Luke 2:11). The words of Isaiah's prophecy were uttered again by the angel foretelling the birth of Jesus in Joseph's prophetic dream: τέξεται δὲ υἱόν (she "will bear [i.e., give birth to, τέξεται] a son," Matt. 1:21-23).

For other births, as in the annunciation to Zachariah of the coming birth of his son John (Luke 1:13), the Gospels use the verb γίγνομαι (*gignomai*). While that verb can certainly refer to birth, it can also mean "come into being." Indeed, γίγνομαι is related to the Greek noun "Genesis," referring to Creation. Accordingly, the verb γίγνομαι is used in John 8:58 in the sense of "be made, be created" when Jesus declares that before Abraham "was made [γενέσθαι], I AM [ἐγώ εἰμι]." Jesus was using the Lord's declaration from the burning bush (Exod. 3:14-15) to indicate His timeless unbounded divinity and His identity as the Creator, and to do this he contrasted himself to Abraham, for the patriarch was of course a human who was exclusively human, a creation of God. In contrast, Jesus is uniquely both fully human and fully divine, and remains the Creator. The diction of the Gospels in recounting the birth of Christ significantly emphasizes the fact of His physical birth by using the unambiguous verb τίκτω (*tikto*) and by not using the equivocal verb γίγνομαι (*gignomai*). Moreover, this diction emphasizes that Jesus was begotten and born; that is, he was not made like Abraham. Thus the Creator is not a creature.

18

Mary and Joseph are referred to as the parents of Christ in the New Testament. The word μήτηρ ("mother") is used of Mary in the New Testament in its full sense of biological birth-giver who is also the one who raised her son. The word "mother" is first used of Mary in Elizabeth's inspired identification of Mary as "mother of my Lord" (Luke 1:43).[57] However, the word "father" is also used of Joseph, to honor his status (Luke 2:33, 48), but without implying any physical contribution on his part to the human nature of Jesus. In the account of the finding of the child Jesus in the Temple (Luke 2:43), Mary and Joseph are identified as His "parents" (γονεῖς, from the verb γίγνομαι), a noun that ordinarily implies biological parenthood. The Holy Spirit did not leave unclear the scriptural basis for the doctrine of the Incarnation, however, for by inspiration the Evangelists elucidated the noun "mother" with references to Mary's actually conceiving and bearing Jesus. Consistently those references use the verb τίκτω (*tikto*).

The first part of the word "Theotokos" is from the Greek noun for "God." The very choice to use the dative Θεῷ (rather than the genitive Θεοῦ) as the first element of the word Θεοτόκος also appears to have been inspired. The dative can have three senses here, and all three are fitting, one each for each Person of the Trinity. When Mary gave birth, the birth she gave was *from* God the Father, and she gave birth *to* God the Son, and this birth was made possible *by means of* God the Holy Spirit. While the genitive case can convey that range of meanings, the use of the dative case gives it more emphasis, and suits better the sense referring to the Holy Spirit.

The second part of the title "Theotokos" is, most fittingly, rooted linguistically in both the prophecy to Isaiah and also the annunciation to Mary. Thus the latter part of the word Θεοτόκος is from τίκτω (*tikto*), the verb indicating biological reproduction. The Early Church's choice of the specific form τόκος (*tokos*) demands our attention. The venerable term Θεοτόκος has been part of Catholic and Orthodox doctrine and worship for seventeen centuries, and so we take the term for granted. Yet it is not what one might have initially expected. After all, at the time of Hippolytus of Rome and later at the Council of Ephesus there had already been for centuries a well-established word for "mother" derived from the verb τίκτω: ἡ τεκοῦσα (*tekousa*), literally, "the one who gives birth, bears [a child]"; the related word for "father," literally, "begetter," is ὁ τεκών (*ho tekon*).[58] Yet the revered word for the Virgin Mary is not Θεουτεκοῦσα, "Mother of God" or "Birther of God." The noun ὁ τόκος, a noun of masculine gender, means "a bringing forth, childbirth, parturition"; by extension, the word can mean "offspring" or "child, son," but not "mother."[59] The word τόκος is construed as "mother" only when it is part of the word Θεοτόκος, and then it means "mother" only by extension, not from strict

---

[57] See also Matt. 2:11, 13, 21; Luke 2:33, 34, 48, 51; John 2:3, 5, 12; 19:25, 27; Acts 1:14.

[58] *An Intermediate Greek-English Lexicon, founded upon the Seventh Edition of Liddell and Scott's Greek-English Lexicon* (Oxford, 1889, reprint 1975) s.v. τίκτω.

[59] Liddell and Scott, *Intermediate Greek-English Lexicon*, s.v. τόκος.

etymology. The startling implication is that, literally, Θεοτόκος appears to mean "Birth of God." Hopefully other scholars will investigate this matter. For the present, let us explore what this implication shows.

d. "Theotokos" as Marian title. Θεοτόκος is, it appears, a venerable title for Mary, the fruit of theological study and mystical contemplation, made authoritative by the Council of Ephesus. It is easy to recognize as titles for Mary the many praises of the Akathistos Hymn, such as "Tabernacle of God the Word," "Key to the Kingdom of Christ," "Ship for those who seek salvation." Θεοτόκος is likewise abstract, having to do with Mary's unique place in salvation history and heaven. In the context of such titles, the title of "Birth of God" has its place.

In mystery, this signal title for Mary calls attention to one way in which the Church needs to be breathing with both lungs, to use a metaphor beloved of Pope John Paul II of blessed memory. For both East and West have by inspiration brought forth profound titles, equally abstract and equally unexpected. Each of these two titles names an event in salvation history, essential to the Incarnation, in which Mary's role is central and absolutely necessary. In each case, the name of the event becomes the title for Our Lady. First came the venerable word Θεοτόκος in the East in the third century. Centuries later came Our Lady's statement at Lourdes, declaring herself to be – not "immaculately conceived" – but the "Immaculate Conception." She is the Immaculate Conception, she is the Birth of God.

We of the East may note that, while the phrasing, "Immaculate Conception," is Western, the inspired recognition is universal within the Church. One need only consider the wealth of ancient and medieval texts "in the various languages of the faithful" that "indicate her purity, in parallel with the purity of Christ the 'immaculate' lamb."[60] She was honored as ἄχραντα in Greek, *immaculata* in Latin, *ungewemmed* in Anglo-Saxon, long before formal affirmation of this doctrine came in 1854.[61] These terms evidently reflect the original scriptural references to the "unspotted" lamb.[62] In most languages the term is expressed negatively: "without spot/blame." In Slavonic, however, it appears that the concept is presented positively and in the superlative: *prečista*, "most pure." This is the word found in the Troparion for the Nativity of Mary, the Kontakion for her Entrance into the Temple, the irmos for the Feast of the Conception of Anne, the prefaces to the irmoi for the Synaxis of Mary on December 26 and for the Dormition, and in several

---

[60] Tkacz, "Reproductive Science and the Incarnation" (as in note 43 above), 12-13.

[61] Catherine Brown Tkacz, "Christian Formulas in Old English Literature: *Naes hyre wlite gewemmed* and Its Implications," *Traditio* 48 (1993) 31-61, at 45-48. For formal affirmation of the Immaculate Conception, see Pius IX, *Ineffabilis Deus*, 1854: DS 2803.

[62] Num. 28:3, 29:17 treat the spotless lamb required for sacrifice; Heb. 9:14 and 1 Pet. 1:19 identify the blood of Christ as that of the spotless lamb. The Church is spotless (Eph. 5:27) and the individual is to seek to remain without spot (2 Pet. 3:14). It was a natural step to recognize Mary as spotless also.

Slavonic Marian hymns.[63] Likewise she is described by the word čísta "pure" in the absolute sense, in which the word itself appears to be understood as superlative.[64] With this abiding Greek and Slavonic tradition of recognizing Mary as prečísta, the title of Immaculate Conception can be embraced as being of the same doctrinally sound nature as the titles for Mary in, for instance, the Akathistos Hymn, and equally well-suited to inspire contemplation of the mystery of the Incarnation.

Among all such titles, the pre-eminent one is Θεοτόκος.

The issue now is whether to translate the term Θεοτόκος. Critical is the fact that the Slavonic liturgy did translate that word. Had the Slavonic liturgy merely transliterated the term Θεοτόκος, the very first English rendering of the Slavonic Divine Liturgy would have simply transliterated it from Cyrillic into the Roman alphabet and brought the word "Theotokos" into the Liturgy as celebrated in English. Instead, however, the Slavonic liturgy translated the word into Slavonic as Bohoróditsa. It may have been Saint Cyril himself who rendered the already-venerable title Theotokos as Bohoróditsa. Certainly Bohoróditsa is an excellent translation of that title, true to its lexical parts: Boho- (like Θεο-) derives from the noun Boh ("God") and róditsa (like τόκος) is from the verb "to give birth to": roditi (like Greek τίκτω).[65] The theological and linguistic achievement of creating the word Bohoróditsa is real. This Slavonic word is part of the liturgical, theological, and cultural heritage of Ruthenians, Ukrainians, Russians, and indeed all Slavs.

The unusual character of the word, both Greek and Slavonic, however, makes it difficult to translate, and various English forms have circulated, including "Godbearer."

e. Analysis of "Godbearer" as a translation of Theotokos / Bohoróditsa. Any translation of Θεοτόκος should resonate with Isaiah's prophecy, the Annunciation, and the other Gospel references to Jesus' birth. Moreover, essential to any worthy translation of Theotokos / Bohoróditsa is unequivocal, absolutely clear reference to the Incarnation. It is on this second point that "Godbearer" falls short. Otherwise, "Godbearer" is in several ways excellent. Like Θεοτόκος, "Godbearer" is cognate with the focal verb indicating the birth of the Lord, for "bear" is the verb in the pertinent passages of Isaiah, Luke, and Matthew in several English translations of the Bible.[66] "Godbearer," however, is potentially ambiguous, for "bear" can mean either "give birth to" or "transport, convey." Our Lady is of course "Godbearer" in both senses, as will be discussed in the next section.

---

[63] *Divine Liturgy* (1978), 91, 101, 106, 114, 141, 157, 158, 159.

[64] See the irmos for the Dormition (ibid., 141) and Marian hymns (157 and 161).

[65] William R. Schmalstieg, *An Introduction to Old Church Slavic*, 2ⁿᵈ ed. rev. and exp. (Columbus, OH: Slavica Publishers, Inc., 1983), 133-36, 227, 273.

[66] "Bear a son" (Is. 7:14), Douai, KJV, RSV, NAB; (Luke 1:31) RSV, NEB (Douai and KJV have "bring forth a son").

21

The main difficulty in translating Θεοτόκος (*Theotokos*) as "Godbearer" is that a different Greek word, Θεοφόρος (*Theophoros*), also means "God-bearer," but not in the unique sense of Θεοτόκος. Unlike the unambiguous τίκτω, the verb φέρω has the same two potential meanings as the English verb "bear," i.e., the sense of a woman bearing (giving birth to) a child, but also the sense of a person transporting or carrying something. It is the latter which is meant by the epithet Θεοφόρος. This designation, Θεοφόρος (*Theophoros*), "Godbearer," "is the traditional honorific of St. Ignatius of Antioch," probably based on his own pastoral use of the term.[67] As a result, also translating Θεοτόκος / *Bohoróditsa* as "God-bearer" can downplay precisely the theological point the original Greek term was designed to emphasize, namely the Incarnation of God, really born of the Virgin Mary.[68]

Another possible English rendering of Θεοτόκος / *Bohoróditsa* is "God-birther." Although that term is free from ambiguity, it is not mellifluous. And it relies on an extended meaning of *tokos* just as much as does the Westernizing designation "Mother of God."

Could, then, "Birth of God" be a fitting English rendering of the Slavonic, as it is of the Greek?

What ought to be the wording in the Divine Liturgy as transmitted through Slavonic and translated into English? There is a great appeal to using, in common with our Greek-speaking brethren, the original Conciliar term Θεοτόκος in at least some of the liturgical texts. Most likely that is the appropriate term to use in the Divine Liturgy. At the same time, because for over a millennium the Divine Liturgy in Slavonic has used *Bohoróditsa*, this strongly indicates that it would be authentic to that tradition to retain that term itself, as venerable. At a minimum, it ought to be occasionally sung in Slavonic hymns; before 2007 our parish sang several Slavonic hymns often, singing first the English translation and then repeating the hymn in Slavonic. Further, it seems advisable to use the Slavic word *Bohoróditsa* in sermons and bulletin inserts and parish website postings on Marian feast days, explaining the history and meaning of the word. It must be noted, however, that these measures are informal and offer no regular use of the historically important term *Bohoróditsa* in the worship of the Metropolia.

Alternatively, since the Slavonic decision was to translate Θεοτόκος, it would be reasonable for any English translation of the Slavonic liturgy also to translate Θεοτόκος / *Bohoróditsa* into English. It would appear that, in order to be consistent with the pattern set in the Gospels and at the Council of Ephesus, this glorious title for Mary ought to be cognate with the verb for giving birth used in the English version of the pertinent passages in the Bible, especially Isaiah 7:14 and Luke 1:31. That is, it appears that a

---

[67] Keleher, "Four Translations of the Divine Liturgy" (as in note 2 above), 302-303.

[68] Ibid., 304, citing Archbishop Jorge Medina Éstevea, Pro-Prefect for the Congregation for Divine Worship and the Discipline of the Sacraments, 1997.

scholarly, orthodox, Catholic English translation of the Septuagint is a prerequisite for rendering this term into English.

f. Further Consideration: The Theotokos and Theosis. In addition, the Mother of God is herself a unique model of theosis.[69] As she physically conceived and gestated and gave birth to God; as she acted such that she was a fitting dwelling place for the Lord, so, the Church Fathers taught, each Christian is to bear the Lord within. This theological tradition is well attested in both East and West. Cyril of Alexandria, Gregory of Nyssa, Maximus the Confessor, and Pseudo-Dionysius, as well as Ambrose, Augustine, Gregory the Great, and many others, taught that we are to "conceive" the Word in our hearts. Mary is also a type of the Church, as noted by several authorities, including Methodius, bishop of Olympos, in his *Symposium*.[70] Richard of St. Victor and Albert the Great were among those who showed how this typology relates to theosis, as when the latter asserted, "The Church gives birth to Christ daily through the faith in the hearts of those who hear the word of God."[71] In the present context it is fitting to call attention to the fact that she is a type of the individual Christian, whether male or female: What she did both spiritually and physically, each Christian is to imitate spiritually. Baptism makes this possible.[72] Anastasius of Sinai described baptism as "generating" new life in likeness of God within the newly baptized.[73] Cyril of Alexandria wrote that "Christ will be formed within us, also, through holiness" and he described this as an "inward birth," and an imitation of Mary.[74] The word θεογενεσία (*Theogenesia*, "birth of God") was used by Pseudo Dionysius the Areopagite to describe what baptism starts within the Christian.[75] Maximus the Confessor describes theosis as imitation of the Mother of God.[76] The same thought is expressed in the Latin West as well, with Ambrose, in his commentary on Luke, exhorting, "Do the will of the Father, that you may be the mother of Christ" (*Fac voluntatem Patris, ut Christi mater sis*).[77] The Feast of the Nativity of the Lord prompted St. Augustine to preach this:

---

[69] The following paragraph is indebted to Hugo Rahner, S.J., "Die Gottesgeburt: Die Lehre der Kirchenvater von der Geburt Christi im Herzen der Glaubigen," *Zeitschrift für Katholische Theologie* 59 (1935):333-418.

[70] Rahner, "Gottesgeburt," p. 364. Also, e.g., Augustine, p. 391.

[71] "Christum parit Ecclesia quotidie per fidem in cordibus auditorum": quoted in Rahner, "Gottesgeburt," p. 399.

[72] Rahner, "Gottesgeburt," pp. 339-53.

[73] Rahner, "Gottesgeburt," p. 372.

[74] Rahner, "Gottesgeburt," p. 371.

[75] Rahner, "Gottesgeburt," pp. 376-77.

[76] Rahner, "Gottesgeburt," pp. 380-81.

[77] Rahner, "Gottesgeburt," p. 388.

What you marvel at in the flesh of Mary, do in the secret places of your soul. The one who with his heart believes in righteousness, conceives Christ. The one who with his mouth confesses salvation, gives birth to Christ. Thus within your minds fecundity may abound and at the same time virginity is sustained.[78]

Eriugena also expressed this theological understanding:

For when one of the faithful undergoes the Sacrament of baptism, what else is accomplished there if not the conception and nativity of the Word of God in his heart, from the Holy Spirit and through the Holy Spirit. Daily, therefore, Christ is conceived and borne and nourished in the womb of faith just as in the loins of [His] most chaste Mother.[79]

It is fitting to find in the venerable titles Theotokos and *Bohoróditsa* the affirmation of Mary's unique role in the Incarnation and also her pre-eminent status as a model of theosis. Such nuances ought to be accessible through whatever way this venerable title for Mary is rendered in the English version of the Divine Liturgy.

It appears that God has entrusted to us, the heirs of the Slavonic tradition, the role in the twenty-first century of giving emphasis to the mystery and meaning of the term Θεοτόκος. This is a complex matter, and one deserving further prayer and study. It would be most fitting to seek the counsel of Mary in prayers addressing her as Theotokos, as *Bohoróditsa*, and perhaps as Birth of God.

Conclusion

As of 2006 the Byzantine Metropolitan Church *Sui Juris* of Pittsburgh has accomplished many salutary restorations, including the profession of the Symbol of Faith without the Latinizing *Filioque* and the practice of giving to newly baptized, chrismated infants the Holy Mystery of the Eucharist. We have also experienced authentic development in hymnody in the form of the new propers for Our Lady of Guadalupe. It is likewise a blessing to have the word "Theotokos" used liturgically, bringing us into uniformity in practice with many of our sister Eastern Churches, both Catholic and Orthodox.

It remains to be seen whether an authentic development of Slavonic worship in English translation will be to use a new, English translation of the Slavonic translation of

---

[78] "Quod miramini in carne Mariae, agite in pentralibus animae. Qui corde credit ad iustitiam, concipit Christum. Qui ore confitetur ad salutem, parit Christum. Sic in mentibus vestris et fecunditas exuberet et virginitas perseveret": quoted in Rahner, "Gottesgeburt," p. 389.

[79] Rahner, "Gottesgeburt," p. 404.

the conciliar Greek title for Mary, *Bohoróditsa*. Whatever is done in this matter must be grounded in the Eastern recognition of the authority of the Greek Old Testament and in the apostolic Slavonic traditions of translation and of transliteration of various liturgically and theologically important words.

Chapter 2:

Principles for Liturgical
Translation and Revision

The commendable goal of giving to the faithful greater unity in the language and music of the liturgy throughout the Metropolia would obviously involve changes. It appears, however, from the liturgical material provided for March 25, 2005, that not merely a few changes are being considered. Rather, a major revision of the entire Ruthenian liturgy in every aspect appears likely, keeping only a very small portion of the materials in use before that date.[80] It is helpful to examine the changes individually and cumulatively. Considered in each of these ways, the changes have implications that are theological, pastoral, poetic, and musical.

It is valuable to recall our context within the whole of the Church and to affirm the distinctive nature of the Ruthenian Rite as a prelude to considering the changes evident in the liturgical materials of March 25, 2005. Some of these changes appear to constitute a new wave of accommodations with the Roman Rite as it is generally practiced in the United States at present. Clearly, changes that tend to Romanize or secularize the Divine Liturgy would only compromise its nature as Slavonic and Catholic.[81]

Our Context

The context for our rite is itself complex. Our rite has its own history, and Eastern Catholics are in special relation to the Orthodox because of our shared liturgical and theological and cultural traditions. Slavonic hymnody itself is a venerable tradition. Our

---

[80] For convenience, in the following pages the prior material will be referred to as, e.g., "in use from at least the 1970s." Although some variations of texts and music exist for those prior materials, nevertheless the publications from the Byzantine Seminary Press and the music leaflets from John Vernoski have an overall consistency and often an exact identity. In the following discussion, some specific liturgical publications will be cited.

[81] The Eastern Church, historically, avoided Protestant influence until recent centuries, but now some Eastern Churches in Western, protestantized countries, are beginning to show influence from non-Catholic theology: Catherine Brown Tkacz, "Iconoclasm, East and West." *New Blackfriars* 85, no. 999 (2004) 542-550. There was, however, a degree of Protestant influence, as in the matter of pietism. An eminent priest of our Metropolia recounts that when, as a child, he had lost a button from his jacket on Sunday, his mother had been sewing it back on, until rebuked by his grandmother for working on Sunday. It appears that his grandmother had been influenced by the Lutheran pietism of her friends and neighbors.

Slavonic translations of the Greek hymns and the original Slavonic chant tones are at least nine hundred years old: Slavonic hymnody consists generally of translations of Greek texts in use in Constantinople ca. 1100, set then to original Slavonic melodies.[82] Considered more broadly, Ruthenian Catholics are part of the whole of Christendom, and we also have important affiliations in faith and practice with Jews, whose worship and sacrifices God transformed into the new worship and sacrifice of His Church.

In the remarks below, reference is made at times to the history of our rite, to its theology, and also to Greek, Slavonic, and the English versions in use from at least the 1970s. The new materials of March 25, 2005, are also compared to those in use by certain other Eastern Catholic, Roman Catholic, and Orthodox Churches, and to other Christian Churches. Both general observations and specific examples are offered in the following discussion. The examples are mainly from Vespers and Divine Liturgy on March 25, 2005. So extremely many changes were present in just these services that it is possible to treat only some here. [Frequent reference to the revised Divine Liturgy has been incorporated, too. This involves considering changes affecting liturgies throughout the church year.[83]]

The Nature of the Byzantine Liturgy

1. *Contemplative*

The Catholic liturgies are the worship of the Church. As such, they also evangelize and catechize and are the medium of contemplation for the faithful.[84] The late Archbishop Joseph Raya wrote with clarity of this: "The liturgy is both a source of theological learning and a form of vital action, for the worship of the Church is centered upon the self-revelation of God to man through the Incarnation of the Son extended in time through sacramental prayer."[85] With a fitting coincidence of dates, the second edition of the *Byzantine Book of Prayer* from which Archbishop Raya is here quoted received the imprimatur on March 25, 1995, precisely a decade before the new version of the Annunciation liturgy used in 2005. Archbishop Raya also explained, "The liturgy is also designed and performed for the people." The "musical, radiant, and penetrating"

---

[82] Kenneth Levy, "The Slavic Kontakia and Their Byzantine Originals," in Queens College Department of Music, *Twenty-Fifth Anniversary Festschrift* (New York, 1964), 79-87, at 82.

[83] [On the use of square brackets in this book, see the third paragraph of the Prologue.]

[84] Rev. William C. Mills makes the same point in "Catechesis through Worship: Education, Formation, Transformation," *Eastern Churches Journal* 10.3 (2003), 29-36.

[85] Archbishop Joseph Raya, "Introduction to the Byzantine Rite," in *Byzantine Book of Prayer*, compiled by the Inter-Diocesan Liturgy Commission of the Ruthenian Metropolitan Province, 2nd ed. (Pittsburgh: Byzantine Seminary Press, 1995), p. xviii.

setting of each liturgy allows the people's experience of worship to "actualize" spiritual realities for them.[86] The Eastern tradition has always recognized that our human nature includes a contemplative capacity and even appetite. Thus, as Archbishop Raya puts it, "The Byzantine liturgy offers to each one the seeds of contemplation he needs."[87] In short, as I have observed elsewhere:

> liturgical texts are designed to be lived with, throughout a lifetime, so that as a worshiper voices a chant over the weeks of its use, and returns to it in that season through the years, it is possible for his understanding of it, and therefore what he personally expresses by singing it, to grow…. Composing a chant is itself the result of reflection and theological meditation, and reciprocally comprehending a chant comes to its singers only as their own reflection and scriptural knowledge grow.[88]

2. *Coherent*

Further, the liturgies of Ruthenian Catholic worship throughout the year are coherent. There are patterns of seasons, of course, the fasts and the feasts, notably the Great Fast and Pascha. Other patterns of coherence permeate the life of a Byzantine Catholic and may go unobserved for years, and then when they dawn on one, the love of God is shown afresh. This coherence is found not only in the propers, but even in some of the ancillary texts and music, that is, in optional hymns and prayers. For instance, the moving hymn *Preterp'ivyj* ("Having Suffered the Passion") chanted throughout the Great Fast is sung to the same music as is the funeral hymn for blessing upon the departed, *Vičnaja pamjat'* ("Eternal Memory"). By this, the Church shows that the death of the faithful occurs within the context of the death and resurrection of Our Lord. It is because God "suffered the Passion for us" that the faithful enjoy "blessed repose and eternal memory." We beseech Him in *Preterp'ivyj* to have mercy, and He does, and therefore the faithful enjoy "blessed repose and eternal memory." Few people may ever notice that the music is identical for these two songs. Noticing is not essential: The music itself is coherent, and that musical coherence is part of Slavonic worship. It is part of why Byzantine worship is experienced as Heaven on earth.

---

[86] Ibid., pp. xviii-xx.

[87] Ibid., p. xxii.

[88] Catherine Brown Tkacz, "Singing Women's Words as Sacramental Mimesis," *Recherches de Théologie et Philosophie Médiévales* 70.2 (2003): 275-328, at 311-312.

3. *Inspired*

The whole liturgical tradition ought to be respected as shaped by the Holy Spirit and as beloved by the faithful. The people need the hierarchy to safeguard this coherence and to protect it from being dismantled, as it has already been dismantled in the contemporary practice of the Roman Rite in America. Vatican II called for the restoration of authentic liturgies, not for wholesale revision of them. One could make a better case for the Bermuda Triangle than for a Vatican II mandate to comprehensively revise the liturgies.[89]

On the Feast day of St. Athanasius, Bishop and Doctor of the Church, Pope John Paul II of blessed memory wrote in affirmation of the *Orientale Lumen* (May 2, 1995), deliberately reiterating the affirmations of Pope Leo XIII in 1895 in *Orientalium Dignitas* and with reference to the documents of Vatican II, especially *Orientalium Ecclesiarum*. Pope John Paul II wrote to "safeguard the significance of the Eastern traditions for the whole Church." He addressed Eastern Catholics as "living bearers of this tradition, together with our Orthodox brothers and sisters." Significantly, he found in the Eastern traditions a freedom from the "voiding of the Cross" evident in some worship. In contrast to the erosions of some worship, the Eastern liturgy continued to aspire to present "heaven on earth," Pope John Paul II wrote, and thereby showed a "great aptitude" for involving the entire human person. With the papal election of Benedict XVI, we have another pope profoundly aware of the integrity of Byzantine worship.

We of the East have preserved authentic traditions of the entire Church while the Roman Rite of recent decades has set aside some of these traditions, such as praying the Creed in the first person singular, "I believe," as it was written (Πιστεύω), with respect for the autonomy of the individual person.[90] In this, we maintain unity with many Catholics throughout the world, including those in Africa and Poland, and with the Orthodox. Similarly, our priests still face East at the altar, leading the whole community, and this coherent liturgical orientation we share with two millennia of Christians of the past. At the start of the new millennium, Josef Cardinal Ratzinger, now Pope Benedict XVI, observed that Byzantine churches maintained continuity in the orientation of the altar.[91] A bright ray of our *Orientale Lumen* is that, with us, our priests symbolically face the rising sun, emblem of the Orient from on high.

---

[89] Father Archimandrite Keleher also doubts that there is adequate basis for the "drastic recasting" proposed: Keleher, *Response to the Proposed Recasting of the Byzantine-Ruthenian Liturgy* (as in note 6 above), e.g., p. 12.

[90] *ΘΕΙΑ ΛΕΙΤΟΥΡΓΙΑ* (as in note 48 above), p. 46.

[91] Josef Cardinal Ratzinger, now Pope Benedict XVI, *The Spirit of the Liturgy*, trans. John Saward (San Francisco: Ignatius Press, 2000). e.g., 76. His constancy in respecting the Byzantine orientation of the priest at the altar as authentic and richly meaningful is seen again in his foreword to U. M. Lang, *Turning Toward the Lord: Orientation in Liturgical Prayer* (Ignatius, 2004).

4. *Focused on Theosis*

Significantly, the doctrine of theosis is conveyed through the Divine Liturgy. The Byzantine Rite has done a faithful job of preserving its distinctive liturgical expression of the purpose of the Incarnation, namely the sanctification of the faithful. This is specifically addressed in *Orientale Lumen*, which praises St. Irenaeus and the Cappadocian Fathers for their perceptive theology of divinization.[92] More effectively than the contemporary Roman Rite in America, the Eastern Churches have continued to convey the idea of divinization. It is necessary that we preserve this affirmation of theosis, not only for the sake of the members of our Metropolia but also for the Catholic Church as a whole, for whom we are to be the Orientale Lumen. From the beginnings our liturgy and our hymnody have been imbued with invitations to seek sanctification.

Notably, the resurrection hymns that are used throughout the year and that invite worshippers to seek sanctification often do so in the words of holy women.[93] In these hymns, as Rev. Thomas Hopko has observed, "Eve is often mentioned together with Adam as rejoicing in the redemption of the human race which together they symbolize."[94] In some of these hymns – including those written by Anatolius (d. 451), Koumoulas, Kosmas the hymnographer (ca. 675-ca. 752) and the Emperor Leo VI (886-912) – the Holy Women at the Tomb are quoted.[95]

5. *Affirmative of Women*[96]

Significantly, women have retained in the Byzantine Church the prominence they gained in Christianity from its inception. Although the basis for this prominence remains in the Roman Catholic Church also, it has had a fuller continuing visibility in the Eastern

---

[92] *Orientale Lumen*, at note 15.

[93] Tkacz, "Singing Women's Words as Sacramental Mimesis," 291-99. Also see Catherine Brown Tkacz, "*Susanna victrix, Christus victor:* Lenten Sermons, Typology, and the Lectionary," *Speculum Sermonis*, ed. Georgiana Donavin, Richard Utz, Cary Nederman (Turnhout: Brepols, 2005), 55-79; and Tkacz, "Women as Types of Christ"

[94] Thomas Hopko, "God and Gender: Articulating the Orthodox View," in *God and Gender,* a special double issue of *St Vladimir's Theological Quarterly* 37 (1993) pp. 141-183 at p. 176.

[95] Tkacz, "Singing Women's Words as Sacramental Mimesis," 298-99, quoting one such hymn by Anatolius.

[96] Extensive detail for this subject is found in Tkacz, "Women and the Church in the New Millennium" (as in note 1 above).

churches. This is largely due to the lesser influence of Protestantism on the Eastern churches.[97]

a. Spiritual equality of the sexes. The East is particularly rich in manifesting the full capacity of both sexes to become holy. This is of course the heritage common to all Christians, because Jesus gave unprecedented emphasis to the spiritual equality of the sexes, and he did so comprehensively.[98] This emphasis began by holy arrangement even in his infancy, for there were male and female witnesses to him both in the womb (Elizabeth and John at the Visitation, Luke 1:42-43) and also in his first appearance in the Temple (Simeon and the prophetess Anna, Luke 2:22-29). This emphasis continued throughout his earthly life, even at its end, as manifest through the steadfast faithfulness of his mother Mary and the disciple John at the foot of Jesus' Cross (John 19:26-27). Consistently, the equal capacity of the male and female human person to do right, to see the truth and to become holy has been affirmed.[99] The Lord in his ministry interacted with both men and women in conversation, in his bestowal of healing and resuscitated life, and in his responsiveness to their intercessory petitions for others.[100] Likewise, professions of faith in him were articulated by both Peter and Martha, and it is notable that Jesus solicited these professions (discussed below). Strikingly, male and female examples recur in the Lord's parables and prophecies, etc. This balanced use of paired sexual examples was innovative; as Tal Ilan notes, such pairs in the haggadah are "really quite rare."[101]

The Lord's emphasis on the spiritual equality of the sexes resulted in a pastoral program of the balanced representation of the sexes beginning in the New Testament Epistles and continuing through the sermons, commentaries, poetry, and visual arts of

---

[97] Tkacz, "Iconoclasm, East and West," as in note 80 above.

[98] Catherine Brown Tkacz, "Jesus and the Spiritual Equality of Women," *Fellowship of Catholic Scholars Quarterly* 24.4 (Fall 2001) 24-29. Useful as a preaching resource, this essay discusses men and women in several Gospels. On women in the Gospels and in the teachings of Jesus, see also Patricia Ranft, *Women and Spiritual Equality in Christian Tradition* (New York: St. Martin's Press, 1998), reviewed in *The University Bookman* 39.2 (Summer 1999) 29-35.

[99] [The fullest presentation of this to date was my illustrated lecture on "Women in the Church," University of Delaware, November 4, 2010, sponsored by the St. Albert Institute for Catholic Thought, the Women's Studies Department and the Philosophy Department. The event was organized by Prof. Katherin A. Rogers, Department of Philosophy.]

[100] For numerous instances, see Tkacz, "Jesus and the Spiritual Equality of Women."

[101] Tal Ilan, *Mine and Yours Are Hers: Retrieving Women's History from Rabbinic Literature* (Leiden: Brill, 1997), 269. Illogically, she doubts the historicity of Jesus' paired examples, but only because other such pairs are occasionally found in antiquity: p. 272, with no examples.

the early and medieval and Byzantine church.[102] Influential expressions of this are the balance of male and female saints in the Church Calendar (notably in the Great Fast and Pascha), in the icons adorning churches (including the pre-eminent pairing of the Theotokos and Christos Pantocrator on the iconostasis), in liturgical prayer, and in so much else. Like Cyril and Methodius, several female saints have been deemed ἰσαπόστολοι ("Equal to the Apostles"), the Holy Women at the Tomb first among them.[103]

b. **Women as types of Christ.** A Christian innovation in biblical exegesis in the first century was to interpret women, as well as men, as prefigurations of Christ. This was a powerful way to demonstrate that women equally with men are called to become holy.[104] These women were pre-eminently Susanna[105] and also Jephthah's daughter, the widow of Zarephath, Judith, Ruth, Esther,[106] and, from the New Testament, the woman in the parable who finds the lost coin and Jairus' daughter. In the East the traditions are particularly strong for Jephthah's daughter, Jairus' daughter, and the woman in the parable, with evidence that formerly there was also a strong Eastern tradition for Susanna as well.[107]

---

[102] Catherine Brown Tkacz, "The Doctrinal Context for Interpreting Women as Types of Christ," *Studia Patristica* 40, ed. Edward Yarnold and Maurice F. Wiles (Oxford University Press, 2006), 253-257.

[103] St. Jerome uses this designation for the three Marys who went to the tomb, which suggests that he learned it from the Divine Liturgy in Jerusalem. Drawing from the Markan account he is explicit that the Lord, rising, first appeared to women ("Dominum resurgentem primum apparuisse mulieribus" -- cf. Mark 16:9: "surgens...apparuit primo Mariae Magdalenae"). Then he states that these women were the apostles of the apostles (*apostolorum illas fuisse apostolas*): *Comm. on Zephaniah* prol. (CCL 76A:671). Other women with this title include the Samaritan woman, known traditionally as S. Photina (lit. "Enlightened Woman"); S. Mariamne, sister of the Apostle Philip; and S. Thekla, disciple of S. Paul: see Tkacz, "Singing Women's Words as Sacramental Mimesis" (as in note 86 above), 297-298.

[104] The fullest presentation of this information to date is my illustrated lecture on "*Susanna victrix, Christus victor*: Old Testament Women as Types of Christ," Blackfriars Hall, Oxford University, February 23, 2010. This lecture was also presented to Bishop White Seminary at Gonzaga University in January, 2010. See also the citations in the following notes.

[105] Catherine Brown Tkacz, "Susanna and the Pre-Christian Book of Daniel: Structure and Meaning," *The Heythrop Journal* 49.2 (2008) 181-196; idem, "ἀνεβόεσεν φωνῇ μεγάλῃ: Susanna and the Synoptic Passion Narratives" (as in note 22 above); idem, "Women as Types of Christ: Susanna & Jephthah's Daughter" (as in note 24 above), pp. 279-92, 308-311; and idem, "Susanna as a Type of Christ," *Studies in Iconography* 29 (1999) 101-53.

[106] Catherine Brown Tkacz, "Esther as a Type of Christ and the Jewish Celebration of Purim," *Studia Patristica* 44 (Leuven: Peeters, 2010) 183-87; see also idem, "Esther, Jesus and Psalm 22," *Catholic Biblical Quarterly* 70.4 (2008) 709-28.

[107] The Byzantine liturgical play, το δραμα της Σωσανίδο (*The Drama of Susanna*), though now lost, is reported by Eustathios of Thessaloniki to treat "how Susanna may show the death of Christ": Kariophiles

Jephthah's daughter has been revered as a type of Christ since antiquity. The earliest known text presenting her as a type (τύπον) of Christ is Greek: S. Methodius, bishop of Olympos, did this in his religious poem, *Symposium*. Other pertinent Greek texts are by Demetrius of Antioch and Procopius of Gaza (ca. 465-ca. 528).[108] The Syriac tradition of this young woman is particularly strong, in, for instance, a Commentary on Judges, wrongly ascribed to Ephrem; in a work by Jacob, bishop of Serug;[109] and in a biblical commentary by Dionysius bar Salībī, the twelfth-century bishop of Amida.[110] Jairus' daughter is a type of Christ in a hymn for Holy Week by Romanos the Melode (d. 555+).[111]

A strong tradition in the East interprets Jesus' parable of the woman who finds the drachma as the Lord's own presentation of her as a type of Christ.[112] Cyril of Alexandria (378-444) may inaugurate this typology in his commentary on the Gospel of Luke.[113] The drachma is a coin stamped with the image (εἰκόνα, icon) of the king, S. Cyril explains, adding, who can doubt that we are the fallen who have been found by Christ? S. John Chrysostom develops this thought in a sermon on this parable, elaborating the lamp in the parable into the lampstand of the Cross with which Christ / the woman found lost humanity.[114] Romanos the Melode in his fourth Kontakion on the Resurrection uses

---

Mitsakis, *Βυζαντινη Υμνογραφια* (Thessalonike: Patriarchikon Idruma Petrikon Meleton, 1971), pp. 330-353, at p. 336. My translation. See also Alessandro d'Ancona, *Origini del teatro Italiano*, 3 books in 2 vols., 2nd ed. (Torini: Ermanno Loescher, 1891), 1:14-15.

[108] *Symposium*, stanza 13, ed. Herbert Musurillo, Sources Chrétiennes 95 (Paris: Éditions du Cerf , 1963), p. 316. All three Greek texts are discussed in Tkacz, "Women as Types of Christ," pp. 293-311, esp. p. 297.

[109] [On these texts by Ephrem and Jacob, see Sebastian Brock, "A *soghitha* on the upright Jephtha and on his daughter, by Mar Isaac," pp. 71-78, esp. at p. 73, an appendix in Susan Harvey and Ophir Münz-Manor, *Jacob of Serug on Jephthah's Daughter: The Metrical Homilies of Jacob of Serug*, Bilingual Syriac-English edition, with introduction and commentary (Gorgias Press, 2010).] Other Syriac traditions make Jephtha himself a type of the Christ, or make him a type of the soul or will of Christ with his daughter being a type of his body, so that together they are a combined type of Christ: See Tkacz, "Women as Types of Christ," 303; [and Brock, "*soghitha*," p. 73 et passim].

[110] For the text, see David Henry Schultze, "The Commentary by Dionysius bar Salibi on the Historical Books of the Old Testament" (Ph.D. diss.: The University of Chicago, 1930), pp. 58-59. The typology is discussed in Tkacz, "Women as Types of Christ," pp. 298-300.

[111] Romanos the Melode, *Hymnes*, 5 vols., ed. Jose Grosdidier de Matons (Paris: Éditions du Cerf, 1964-81), vol. 4, pp. 392-95; *Kontakia of Romanos, Byzantine Melodist*, 2 vols., tr. Marjorie Carpenter (Columbia, Miss.: University of Missouri Press, 1970, 1973) vol. 1, pp. 317-18. Discussed in Catherine Brown Tkacz, "Recovering the Tradition: Women as Types of Christ," article in submission, at pp. 57-58 of typescript.

[112] Detailed in Tkacz, "Recovering the Tradition," pp. 59-63.

[113] S. Cyril of Alexandria, *Commentarium in Lucam* 15.8 (PG 72:800-1).

[114] S. John Chrysostom, in PG 61:781-84: see also Grosdidier, *Hymnes*, vol. 4, pp. 570-571.

John's treatment, adding more scriptural language.[115]

The Church, East and West, has largely presented women as types of Christ to the faithful through preaching. Mainly in the West this was supplemented by visual depictions of men and women as types of Christ from antiquity through the sixteenth century.[116] At the same time, universally the Church's liturgies proper have always conveyed coherent affirmation of the capacity of everyone, male and female, to attain holiness.

Whatever changes may be introduced into the Ruthenian Liturgy, they ought not to weaken or undercut its character as contemplative, coherent, inspired, focused on theosis and affirmative of women.

Principles for change

Principles for biblical and liturgical translation are evident in the history of Christian biblical and liturgical translation, notably in the work of St. Jerome on the Bible and in the translators of our Slavonic hymnody into the English in use at least since the 1970s. Moreover, the Church since Vatican II has set forth clear instructions for such translation and for liturgical renewal and preservation. Before turning in detail to the Vatican Instruction, augmented by reference to St. Jerome and to our Slavonic translations, it is useful to set forth a simple, basic principle: The new must be better than the old.

1. *The new must be better than the old.*

Major change requires major work to implement it. Far more importantly, major changes in liturgical and biblical texts and musical settings mean that the faithful will lose what they have memorized. They must learn something quite different before they can pray it as they have been able to pray the old. If the changes are wide-sweeping, as it appears the changes could be in the Metropolia, then many of the elderly will not live long enough to memorize the new. We must be very sure that the new is worth the personal sacrifice asked of the faithful. The new cannot simply be "as good as" the old. It must be better, or it is merely change for change's sake. "Change" in the abstract is morally neutral. "Restoration" and "authentic development" are holy and therefore good. Any new liturgical or biblical texts and music must, individually and together, be better than the old, and they must be better not just in one aspect, but comprehensively: theologically, poetically, and musically.

---

[115] Romanos the Melode, *Hymnes* vol. 4, pp. 577-581: see also Carpenter, *Kontakia of Romanos,* vol. 1, p. 284.

[116] Catherine Brown Tkacz, "*O Beatissima Susanna:* Three Witnesses in the Walters to an Articulate Woman in Iconographic Context," *Journal of the Walters Art Museum* (forthcoming).

The example of St. Jerome comes to mind. When in the fourth century he was correcting the Latin translation of the Gospels (the start of his work on the whole Bible), he wrote to Pope Damasus that unless there was a compelling reason to change a word, or even the order of words, he did not change them:

> Some passages were not very far in meaning from the customary Latin rendering. I commanded my pen that, when it had corrected those which seemed to change the true sense, it should allow the others to remain as they had been.[117]

If the meaning required a change, he would make it. But otherwise, he respected the fact that the faithful loved the very words in which they had been praying, perhaps for all of their lives. Put simply: Although he changed what he had to, he didn't tinker.

2. *Liturgiam Authenticam*

Happily, the Church has provided a clear Instruction on the renewal and preservation of *Liturgiam Authenticam*, the authentic worship of the Church.[118] This instruction is a document of great timeliness and value.[119] The Eastern rites (§§ 4, 90) and the authority of the Septuagint (§ 41b-c) are treated in this Vatican document issued in 2001. Specifically, it echoes the Second Vatican Council in asking that the traditions of each of the Eastern rite Churches "be preserved whole and intact."

---

[117] "Quae ne multum a lectionis latinae consuetudine discreparent, ita calamo imperavimus ut, his tantum quae sensusm videbantur mutare correctis, reliqua manere pateremur ut fuerant," Jerome's *Preface to the Gospels*, lines 30-32, my translation. For more on Jerome's work on the Bible, see my essays "*Labor tam utilis*: The Creation of the Vulgate" (as in note 19 above), and "Ovid, Jerome, and the Vulgate," *Studia Patristica* 33 (1996): 378-382.

[118] "*Liturgiam Authenticam*: On the use of Vernacular Languages in the Publication of the Books of the Roman Liturgy," Fifth Instruction "For the Right Implementation of the Constitution on the Sacred Liturgy of the Second Vatican Council (*Sacrosanctum Concilium*, art. 36), by the Congregation for Divine Worship and the Discipline of the Sacraments, issued 28 March 2001. A valuable introduction to this document is Helen Hull Hitchcock, "A New Era in the Renewal of the Liturgy: The Holy See Issues Its 'Fifth Instruction' Implementing the Vatican II Liturgical Reforms," *The Catholic Imagination: Proceedings from the Twenty-Fourth Annual Convention of the Fellowship of Catholic Scholars, Omaha, Nebraska, September 28-30, 2001*, ed. Kenneth D. Whitehead (South Bend: Saint Augustine's Press, 2003), 143-50; see also and Raymond T. Gawronski, "When Beauty is Revolutionary: Reflections on *Liturgiam Authenticam*," in *Catholic Imagination*, 159-68. Father Gawronski, in addition to being a member of the Philosophy faculty at Marquette University, is an aggregate member of Mount Tabor Byzantine Catholic Monastery at Redwood Valley, California.

[119] *Pace* Robert F. Taft, S.J., *Through Their Own Eyes: Liturgy as the Byzantines Saw It* (Berkeley: InterOrthodox Press, 2006), p. 5.

The Second Vatican Ecumenical Council in its deliberations and decrees assigned a singular importance to the liturgical rites, the ecclesiastical traditions, and the discipline of Christian life proper to those particular Churches, especially of the East, which are distinguished by their venerable antiquity, manifesting in various ways the tradition received through the Fathers from the Apostles. The Council asked that the traditions of each of these particular Churches be preserved whole and intact. For this reason, even while calling for the revision of the various Rites in accordance with sound tradition, the Council set forth the principle that only those changes were to be introduced which would foster their specific organic development.[120]

While this Instruction treats the Roman Liturgy primarily, it is directly pertinent to the proposed changes in the Divine Liturgy. To be explicit, the misapplication of Vatican II to the Roman Rite is the subject of *Liturgiam Authenticam*, and what is proposed in the Ruthenian Rite now is, in the main, a parallel misapplication of Vatican II. Rather than promulgate in the Divine Liturgy the errors of recent praxis in the Roman Rite, it would be far better to avoid committing the same mistakes in the Divine Liturgy. Historically, the membership in Ruthenian churches in the United States increased after the post-Vatican II changes in the Roman Rite, with many devout Catholics who wanted to worship reverently themselves and who wanted a reverent worship for their children's sake becoming Ruthenian. This certainly suggests that such members of the churches may again migrate if the Divine Liturgy now becomes Americanized.[121]

Importantly, this Instruction affirms principles of translation and revision that clearly pertain to every rite and that are most apt for the present situation in the Ruthenian Catholic Church in this country. Moreover, these principles are themselves traditional, for they are evident in the work of that famous biblical translator, St. Jerome, and they are again often evident in the translations of our Ruthenian liturgy in use for decades. This agreement of *Liturgiam Authenticam* with both a Doctor of the Church and with the particular tradition of the Ruthenian Rite is an instance of the unifying guidance of the Holy Spirit.

It is worth emphasizing once more that the Slavic tradition comes from the apostolic work of SS. Cyril and Methodius, ἰσαπόστολοι ("Equal to the Apostles"). We are Greek Catholic; we are also specifically Slavic Catholic.

a. Respect the right of the faithful to memorized, contemplative worship. Strikingly, the faithful are central in this Instruction. *Liturgiam Authenticam* returns again and again to the importance of the faithful, maintaining that, for their sake, the liturgy ought to be free of unneeded changes. Great respect is shown for the active faith and

---

[120] *Liturgiam Authenticam* § 4, citing the Second Vatican Council, Const. *Sacrosanctum Concilium,* § 4; Decr. *Orientalium Ecclesiorum,* §§ 2, 6.

[121] [Indeed, it appears that throughout the Metropolia parishes whose administrators use exclusively the revised *Divine Liturgy* have seen members become Melkites or Orthodox, etc.]

intelligence of the laity. For instance, it is recognized that the faithful pay attention to the words of the liturgy, reflect on them, memorize them, and pray with them. Thus does the liturgy supply what Archbishop Raya termed "the seeds of contemplation."

Respect for the laity motivates *Liturgiam Authenticam* to affirm that it is of "greatest importance" that the biblical translations ought to be uniform and stable, "In order that the faithful may be able to commit to memory at least the more important texts of the Sacred Scriptures and be formed by them even in their private prayer."[122] The liturgical translations ought to be characterized by "a certain stability" whenever possible. "The parts that are to be committed to memory by the people, especially if they are sung, are to be changed only for a just and considerable reason."[123] It is notable that the Eucharistic prayers are specifically addressed, although of course they are neither sung nor spoken by the people. The Congregation for Divine Worship, and Pope John Paul II, who authorized the promulgation of *Liturgiam Authenticam*, recognized that the Eucharistic prayers as so important to the faithful that a paragraph of the Instruction is devoted to these prayers: "Without real necessity, successive revisions of translations should not notably change the previously approved vernacular texts of the Eucharistic Prayers *which the faithful will have committed gradually to memory*."[124] The document then refers to the same principles it gives regarding the people's sung portions of the liturgy. Our Byzantine Council of Hierarchs has shown the same respect for the prayerful participation of the laity in the Divine Liturgy when the Council restored the singing of "To You, O Lord" to its shorter version so that the faithful could hear the words of the celebrant's prayer.[125]

b. Retain liturgical style and language. The Church in *Liturgiam Authenticam* advises its pastors not to rush to simplify biblical and liturgical texts into what they "really mean," as if mode of expression and metaphor were extraneous. Repeatedly the need for both accessibility and integrity is affirmed. For instance:

> While it is permissible to arrange the wording, the syntax and the style in such a way as to prepare a flowing vernacular text suitable to the rhythm of popular prayer, the original text, insofar as possible, must be translated integrally and in the most exact manner.[126]

---

[122] *Liturgiam Authenticam* § 36.

[123] *Liturgiam Authenticam* § 74.

[124] *Liturgiam Authenticam* § 64, italics mine.

[125] Praised above, at p. 13.

[126] *Liturgiam Authenticam* § 20, citing documents from 1967 and 1997. This instruction continues, "without omissions or additions in terms of their content, and without paraphrases or glosses. Any adaptation to the characteristics or the nature of the various vernacular languages is to be sober and discreet."

Again:

> So that the content of the original texts may be evident and comprehensible even to the faithful who lack any special intellectual formation, the translations should be characterized by a kind of language which is easily understandable, yet which at the same time preserves these texts' dignity, beauty, and doctrinal precision. By means of words of praise and adoration that foster reverence and gratitude in the face of God's majesty, his power, his mercy and his transcendent nature, the translations will respond to the hunger and thirst for the living God that is experienced by the people of our own time, while contributing also to the dignity and beauty of the liturgical celebration itself.[127]

To this we of the Slavic Rite add that our Apostles, SS. Cyril and Methodius, named the new faithful "Slavs," from *slava* "glory." The beauty of the Slavonic liturgy is imbued with glory and is not mundane.

Insightfully, *Liturgiam Authenticam* clarifies that "sacred style" is distinct from ordinary speech and that liturgical texts are to be "free of an overly servile adherence to prevailing modes of expression." This Instruction continues with another affirmation of the importance to the faithful of having a liturgy that can be committed to memory:

> If indeed, in the liturgical texts, words or expressions are sometimes employed which differ somewhat from usual and everyday speech, it is often enough by virtue of this very fact that the texts become truly memorable and capable of expressing heavenly realities. Indeed, it will be seen that the observance of the principles set forth in this Instruction will contribute to the gradual development, in each vernacular, of a sacred style that will come to be recognized as proper to liturgical language.[128]

The faithful do in fact recognize this style in the English version of the Ruthenian Catholic Liturgy in use since at least the 1970s. What is stated next in the Instruction describes what has in fact already happened in our rite:

> Thus it may happen that a certain manner of speech which has come to be considered somewhat obsolete in daily usage may continue to be maintained in the liturgical context. In translating biblical passages where seemingly inelegant words or expressions are used, a hasty tendency to sanitize this characteristic is likewise to be avoided. These principles, in fact, should free

---

[127] *Liturgiam Authenticam* § 25.

[128] *Liturgiam Authenticam* § 27.

the Liturgy from the necessity of frequent revisions when modes of expression may have passed out of popular usage.[129]

Indeed, respecting the value of sacred style in the liturgy is essential not only for authentic worship: Sacred style is also needed so that the faithful may have a mode of prayerful expression which in turn is available to them in their daily lives and in their proper influence upon culture. As the Instruction observes, "liturgical prayer not only is formed by the genius of a culture, but itself contributes to the development of that culture."[130] A woman of our parish expressed the same insight: "The culture flows from the liturgy to the people, not the other way."[131]

Vocabulary and syntax are each treated at length in *Liturgiam Authenticam*.[132] Many liturgical texts must be "suitable for being set to music."[133] "By their very nature," the Instruction observes, liturgical texts are intended "to be proclaimed orally and to be heard in the liturgical celebration" and thus "they are characterized by a certain manner of expression that differs from that found in ordinary speech." This manner often features "recurring and regular patterns of syntax and style, a solemn or exalted tone, alliteration and assonance, concrete and vivid images, repetition, parallelism and contrast, a certain rhythm, and at time, the lyric of poetic compositions."[134]

Sometimes it is not possible, of course, to replicate in a translation all the features of the original. This has always been true: In the fourth century St. Jerome observed that the Hebrew acrostics in Lamentations 1-4 could not be identically reproduced in Latin, so he used Latin metrics to convey the poetic nature of the passage. Moreover, from his letters, commentaries, and the prefaces he wrote to the individual books of the Bible it is clear that throughout his project of revision and fresh translation of the Bible, St. Jerome was sensitive to its style, syntax, genres, poetic techniques, and tone, in Hebrew, Aramaic, Greek, and Latin. [135] He proceeded, we know from his letters and commentaries, in exactly the manner the Church prescribes in the 2001 Instruction:

---

[129] *Liturgiam Authenticam* § 27.

[130] *Liturgiam Authenticam* § 47.

[131] Mrs. Margaret (Peggy) Baird made these remarks when regretting and objecting to the March 25, 2005, elimination of "Lover of Mankind," in favor of politically correct forms such as "Lover of humanity."

[132] *Liturgiam Authenticam* section 3A: Vocabulary, §§ 49-56, section 3B: Syntax, style and literary genre, §§ 57-62.

[133] *Liturgiam Authenticam* § 60.

[134] *Liturgiam Authenticam* § 59.

[135] Tkacz, *"Labor tam utilis"* (as in note 19 above), 42-44.

The translator should seek to ascertain the intended effect of such elements in the mind of the hearer as regards thematic content, the expression of contrast between elements, emphasis and so forth. Then he should employ the full possibilities of the vernacular language skillfully in order to achieve as integrally as possible the same effect as regards not only the conceptual content itself, but the other aspects as well. In poetic texts, greater flexibility will be needed in translation in order to provide for the role played by the literary form itself in expressing the content of the texts. Even so, expressions that have a particular doctrinal or spiritual importance or those that are more widely known are, insofar as possible, to be translated literally.[136]

These principles are universal, and they have in fact been followed by those in the past who, like St. Jerome, have approached liturgical and biblical translation with skill and acumen both theological and literary.

A related point can be made. Christians created new words in Greek and then later in Latin as well to express new Christian experiences and doctrines. The words "Christian" and "Trinity" were among these newly minted terms. One new term of great importance was created to express the doctrine that God became Man: *ensarkosis* (also *sarkosis*, based on John 1:14, the Word became *sarx* "flesh"). That term is part of the Nicene Creed (*sarkothenta*) and is rendered as *incarnatio* in Latin. As Dr. Christine Mohrmann showed in the 1970s, Christians also wanted to distinguish their worship of the one true God by using language distinctive from the words of pagan worship, and therefore Christians invented new versions of religious words (e.g., Latin *glorificare* to be distinct from *gloriare*). They also coined the Greek word *apocalypsis* to denote the new Revelation.[137] Recently it has also been shown that the early Christians also invented the corresponding Latin neologism, *revelatio* and, for contrast, the new word *velatio*, to indicate the hidden meaning of various types before Christ's Incarnation made their meaning intelligible.[138] Given this sensitivity to the words of worship, it is notable that Christians also retained certain Hebrew words as venerable and rich in holy associations, e.g., *Alleluia, Amen, Hosanna,* as well as *Pâsach,* which in Greek and Slavonic became *Pascha.* This language shows the continuity of the new Christian revelation with the original revelation to the Jews. Use of these Hebrew terms allows the faithful through the ages to honor God and His mysteries with the same words of worship used as far back as history records.

---

[136] *Liturgiam Authenticam* § 59.

[137] For instance, she showed that Christians invented new versions of religious words (e.g., *glorificare,* and other verbs with -*fic*- inserted) to distinguish the new, true worship from paganism, and also coined the word *apocalypsis: Études sur le latin des chrétiens,* 4 vols. (Rome: Edizioni di Storia e Letteratura, 1958-65) 4:20.

[138] Catherine Brown Tkacz, "*Velatio,*" in *Saint Augustine through the Ages: an Encyclopedia,* ed. Allan Fitzgerald (Grand Rapids: William B. Eerdmans Publishing Company, 1999).

A Slavic example of such fine translation work is useful to consider. The text treated here, "Today the sacred Pasch is revealed to us," one of the Paschal stichera, exemplifies the quality of translation generally found in the liturgy in use since at least the 1970s.[139] Greek and Slavonic are highly inflected languages, but modern English is not. As a result, Slavonic and Greek can express complex ideas more concisely than English. For instance, the celebrant's exclamation, "Holy things for the holy," is simply two words in the Slavonic: "*Svataja svjatym!*"[140] The English cannot, perhaps, be merely "Holy holy!" because that would be ambiguous and confusing. Word order is also affected by difference in language: Modern English translations of Greek and Slavonic liturgical and hymn-texts must at times alter the word order of the inflected original to make intelligible English. In Slavonic, and presumably in the Greek original, the hymn "Today the sacred Pasch" consists of ten statements, each one beginning with the word "Pasch."[141] This word is the same in Greek and in Slavonic, and is simply the Greek transliteration of the Hebrew *pâsach*, 'Passover.'[142] Some of the statements in the Slavonic omit the form of "to be" in order to be more emphatic: For instance, "*Pascha Christos izbavitel'*" and "*Pascha virnych.*" It is quite likely that the Greek original also omits any form of "to be," so that here again the Slavonic translator retained the poetic and rhetorical pattern of the Greek. The important theological term in the final sentence points to the whole purpose of the Incarnation, i.e., the sanctification of the faithful. Indeed, this paschal sticheron builds to joyous adoration of "the Pasch which sanctifies all the faithful."[143] The key term of theosis, "sanctifies," is here given its traditional, direct Slavonic equivalent, linguistically analogous to the Greek, for the word "holy" (*svyat*) is its root: *osvajaščajuščaja*. In English this term is aptly and clearly rendered "sanctifies." The Slavic for "sanctification" is also found in, e.g., the Litany of Thanksgiving, "For you are our sanctification (*osvajaščenije*)."[144] The same word is used of the Eucharistic

[139] For the English and Slavonic, see *Matins of the Resurrection with Music for the Divine Liturgy and Blessing the Paschal Food* (Pittsburgh: Byzantine Seminary Press, 1976), 38. The cover title of this booklet is *Resurrection Matins*, the title used hereafter in these notes. In my research I have compared various Greek hymns and prayers to the Slavonic translation of them: See esp. Tkacz, "Singing Women's Words as Sacramental Mimesis" (as in note 86 above), passim. While I have not seen the particular Greek hymn discussed here, it seems highly likely that the same pattern evident in other Slavonic translations applies here, namely that the emphasis by initial position throughout this hymn comes from the Greek original.

[140] For the Slavonic, see *Divine Liturgy* (1978), 24.

[141] Very similar, evidently the source of the hymn still in use, is the Easter Communion hymn used in Jerusalem in antiquity. It is ascribed to St. John of Damascus in Lavra Ms Γ.67, fol. 47r, a musical codex of the tenth or eleventh century, in Chartres notation: Dimitri Conomos, "Communion Hymns," *St. Vladimir's Theological Quarterly* 25.2 (1981): 95-122, at 114-116.

[142] Tkacz, "Singing Women's Words as Sacramental Mimesis," 286, and Schmalstieg, *Old Church Slavic* (as in note 64 above), 264.

[143] For the English and Slavonic, see *Resurrection Matins*, 38.

[144] *Divine Liturgy* (1978), 27.

elements which are "consecrated" (*osvajaščennych*) and likewise Mary is described as the "sanctified" (*osvajaščennyj*) Temple.[145]

The translator into Slavonic respected both the word "Pascha" and the word for theosis as expressions having "a particular doctrinal or spiritual importance"[146] and therefore prudently rendered them carefully, transliterating the first and translating the second literally. Also, the translator did well to use normal English syntax for this hymn, although as a result no statement in the English begins with the word "Pasch." The translation, however, effectively conveys the richly concentrated celebration of the mystery of what the Pasch is. It was also a pastorally sound decision to vary the word "Pasch" with "Passover" as a way of showing that the words are synonyms. In sum, the translation of that hymn is pastoral, intelligent, effective, and a coherent part of worship. The translator, relying on prayer, theology, and common sense, fully met the criteria of the 2001 Instruction *Liturgiam Authenticam* decades before it was written, just as St. Jerome had done many centuries earlier.

3. *Principles Specific to the Ruthenian Rite.*

An additional pair of principles apply to the Ruthenian Rite, because of its layered linguistic history. That is, the Ruthenian Rite is a translation from the Greek, and the Slavonic translation itself has an authority. Moreover, its chant was created for the Divine Liturgy in Slavonic. Finally, the Slavonic Liturgy has itself been translated into English, more than once, and these versions ought to be taken into account in preparing any new materials.

a. Respect the validity of the Slavonic. Differences between Slavonic and Greek ought to be respected. The Slavonic is neither negligible nor irrelevant. To the contrary, it is part of our authentic heritage. S. Cyril was inspired to achieve the translation of the Bible and of the Divine Liturgy and other liturgical and hymn-texts into Slavonic, and he personally translated the Psalter and the New Testament.[147] These Slavonic translations must be examined as authentic and potentially apostolic. As stated above, when the Slavonic liturgy is translated into English, the Slavonic ought not to "wash out" as if it were irrelevant and only the Greek matters. Both must be honored, if the integrity of the rite is to be maintained.

As far as possible, the Slavonic pattern regarding whether a term is transliterated or translated should be followed in English, for instance. That is, the fact that the Greek term Θεοτόκος was translated into Slavonic as *Bohoróditsa* strongly indicates that ideally

---

[145] *Divine Liturgy* (1978), 21, 101.

[146] *Liturgiam Authenticam* (as in note 36 above) § 59.

[147] Paul A. Hollingsworth, "Constantine the Philosopher (monastic name Cyril)," *ODB* (as in note 47 above), 1:507.

English would also translate this term, or at the very least keep the term current in catechesis and preaching. In parishes where it is not already current, a goal should be to make the term known. Also, since the term Θεοφιλεστάτου was translated into Slavonic specifically as *bohol'ubiv'im*, "God-loving" (see below), any English version of the Liturgy ought to respect that and render the term accurately according to the Slavonic.

Moreover, repristination is properly prior to reform, as Father Archimandrite Keleher has pointed out, and one notes that this view is shared by the eminent Byzantine liturgiologist Archimandrite Robert F. Taft, S.J., who cites the need "to recover the integrity of the pristine tradition" in order to serve present pastoral needs.[148] In this regard, the present need is first to implement the full Ruthenian Recension rather than drastically to overhaul an English version that is not based on it.

The *Recensio Rutena* of the Divine Liturgy was promulgated by Rome in 1941 and reprinted in Užhorod in 1944, but the difficulties of wartime communication delayed even the communication of this recension to the Pittsburgh Metropolitanate.[149] Although in 1954 implementation of the Ruthenian Recension was begun by Bishop Daniel Ivancho, when he retired later that year the process was halted. Even today, "The majority of the faithful of the parishes of the Pittsburgh Metropolitanate have probably never had an opportunity to attend the Divine Liturgy served in accordance with the official service books."[150]

b. Compare prior English translations. As Jerome was well aware, sometimes a translator has before him a text that is itself a translation of an earlier one, as the Old Latin and Greek versions of the Old Testament he used for comparison were themselves translations from Hebrew.[151] Jerome worked directly from the Hebrew, but used the other versions as comparanda.[152] Regarding the pre-1976 English translations of Slavonic liturgical texts, the likelihood should be taken into account that they were made by persons who to some extent knew both the Slavonic and also the Greek texts which were the basis of the Slavonic. It is entirely possible, for instance, that the English translators may have understood techniques of Greek hymnody and therefore sought to use those techniques in the English translations, even in cases where the Slavonic itself could only represent those techniques in part. That is, it seems reasonable that our third-millennial

---

[148] Keleher, *Response to the Proposed Recasting of the Byzantine-Ruthenian Liturgy* (as in note 6 above), p. 11; Taft, "Liturgy in the Life of the Church" (as in note 33 above), 203.

[149] Keleher, op. cit., pp. 11, 21, 73-74. Somewhat later an additional *Ordo Celebrationis* came from Rome: pp. 24ff, 30. For a full, detailed and documented discussion of the Ruthenian Recension, see Father Archimandrite Keleher's monograph.

[150] Keleher, op. cit., p. 40.

[151] Except, of course, for those parts of the Old Testament composed in Aramaic or Greek, such as the Books of Maccabees.

[152] Tkacz, "*Labor tam utilis*" (as in note 19 above), passim.

review of English translations of Slavonic liturgical texts should look at both the Slavonic and also at the original Greek.

Conclusion

Five principles have been adduced in this chapter. First, and over-riding all, is the Golden Rule of liturgical reform and revision, namely, the new must be better than the old. Next, respect for the spiritual life of the faithful requires that no impediment to their experience of the liturgy in the form of depriving them of memorized texts is to be introduced unless absolutely necessary. If a text had been translated in a heretical way, for instance, that would make its retranslation essential. There is no evidence, however, of any such problem with the English in use for decades, through 2006. Moreover, the style and language of the liturgy in translation should be consonant with that in the original. The liturgy is not a menu in a fast food restaurant, to be taken in at a glance; it is the celebration of the mystical supper, and it will take the faithful a lifetime to drink in its fullness. Two further principles apply to the Ruthenian Rite. First, and quite importantly, the Slavonic worship is itself valid, not merely a transient version of the Greek. SS. Cyril and Methodius the Church has proclaimed as equal to the Apostles, and the apostolic weight of their liturgy is real. Finally, analysis of the prior English versions of the Slavonic is an appropriate part of working on any revision or on a new English version.

Chapter 3:

Analysis of the Liturgical
Materials of March 25, 2005

Certainly the materials of March 25, 2005 are different.[153] Changes are introduced on virtually every page and often in every line. The texts of the Divine Liturgy and of Matins and of Vespers are changed, the texts of the proper hymnody are changed, the texts of the biblical translations, which are staples of the people's prayed song, are changed. Such radical and extensive revision is profoundly distracting to the faithful. If the new materials were better than the ones already in use, such change would be worthwhile. A few changes are excellent. But the new materials are very, very often less good in quality. Often they are poor. Where they are good, it is frequently by virtue of having retained enough of the prior version to be so. [Regrettably, these problems characterize the revised Divine Liturgy as a whole.[154]]

Most seriously, many changes alter the theology. Happily, it seems likely that the theological changes were inadvertent, rather than a decision to minimize certain doctrines, such as theosis. However, it is disturbing that such changes appear therefore to have been made accidentally. Positive changes are the introduction of the word "Theotokos," the revision of "testament" to "covenant" in the anaphora, the improved layout, and a few other items. Except for these, however, the prior liturgy was superior theologically, poetically, and musically.

Although surely it was unintentional, the music of March 25, 2005, introduced several changes which show disregard of the faithful and their role in the liturgy. The liturgy is worship performed by the entire community, with celebrant, deacon, servers, cantor, and the faithful acting harmoniously, with distinct, well-integrated roles and specific liturgical actions. Regrettably, in the musical materials of March 25, 2005, it is as if the role of the faithful has been deemed of little importance. For instance, where the cantors are to set the musical line so that the faithful can then sing a proper hymn in that

---

[153] They may be available as a download from the website of the Metropolitan Cantor Institute: http://metropolitancantorinstitute.org/. Regarding the entire revised Divine Liturgy, promulgated in 2007, it would of course be useful to analyze the rubrics and the texts assigned to the celebrant as well as the texts assigned to the congregation and cantors.

[154] [On the use of square brackets in this book, see the third paragraph of the Prologue.]

tone readily, instead the cantor lines are now different from what the faithful sing.[155] That is, the introductory section sung by the cantor often sets the pattern to be followed in the portion sung by the faithful. On March 25, Tone 2 was frequently used at Vespers, and the cantor's opening should set the cadence in this way.

A member of the Intereparchial Music Commission graciously reviewed that point with me, in a way greatly to his credit. He began by stating that my point was mistaken: He asserted that the *pripiv*, the introductory sticheron, does not have the purpose of introducing the cadence, and that the opening musical lines do not set the pattern. To demonstrate this, he proposed to sing each of the eight tones from Bokshai's edition.[156] As soon as he had sung Tone 2, however, he paused and acknowledged that in that case the *pripiv* matched the cadence of the tone as a whole. I honor him for continuing to chant the remaining tones and for observing without hesitation that for at least Tones 4 and 7, again, the *pripiv* provided a pattern for the portion to be sung by the faithful.[157] On a prior occasion as well, when I had remarked to him on the meaningful musical parallel between two important passages (*Preterp'ivyj* and *Vičnaja pamjat*, discussed above), he asked me to sing them. Then he agreed that the parallel was present and added that he had not been aware of it before.

His remarks show that the IEMC introduced changes into the music of the *pripiv* of Tone 2 without having recognized one of its functions. This is, they vitiated a function they had not even known existed. It is entirely reasonable that a few individuals, even ones deeply concerned with the music of the Liturgy, would not be aware of all of its musical complexity and richness. That fact, however, should make them, and the hierarchs, cautious about introducing any and every change. Respect for the liturgy and respect for the faithful indicate that such caution is prudent.

It is useful to look in detail at the changes.

Layout

The layout of materials is quite successful. It certainly deserves praise. The visual clarity of the materials is also very good indeed. Presumably a software for producing musical scores was used. The results are most readable. The font, its size, and the clarity and size of the musical notes were well selected. Also, both in the continued use of already familiar layout and in the introduction of slight changes, the presentation was

---

[155] Mrs. Margaret Baird, cantor, observed this very quickly while preparing for the celebration of the Divine Liturgy on March 25, 2005. Detailed comparison of the prior musical settings to the new ones confirmed her observation.

[156] Ioann V. Bokshai and Iosif I. Malinich, *V Mukachevskoi grek. kaf. eparkhii ustanoviennoe Tserkovnoe prostopienie* [score] (Ungvar: Unio, 1906).

[157] My notes on his remarks on Tone 6 are incomplete; this tone also may set the pattern.

effective. Continuing the practice of enclosing alternate musical settings in boxes made it easy both to distinguish between the options and also to identify swiftly the next portion of the liturgy.

Particularly well thought and well done was the addition of the simple indicators "Cantor" and "All." This discreet change was an excellent enhancement to the layout in our existing Great and Holy Week music booklets. The presentation of the antiphonal psalms, with italics marking the syllable on which to change notes, was also clear. Again, that slight change, using italics as cue, was completely effective and most welcome.

Rubrics

Considered here are only those rubrics in the limited materials of March 25, 2005; comments on twenty-six rubrical problems in the proposed recasting of the Divine Liturgy have been offered by Father Archimandrite Keleher, who notes that a twelve-word phrase has been inserted into one, from no known source.[158] Generally, of course, most of the italicized comments and directions in the materials of March 25, 2005, were taken from earlier liturgical materials. However, some of the rubrics were new. All the new ones are problematic. Specifically, unnecessary remarks were inserted within texts, thus tending to disrupt the prayer. Also, one rubric shows a surprising ignorance of Eastern liturgy.

The texts of the liturgy, its psalms and prayers, ought to be presented to the clergy and the faithful as these texts exist now. It is pedantic and intrusive to interrupt psalms or prayers with obscure comments intended (I surmise) to mark the ancient subparts of the texts. It is distracting to inject "And again" before the conclusion of a psalm as it is sung today.[159]

Quite poor in this regard are the injected remarks and odd layout for the Communion Prayer, *Pisteuo, Kyrie* ("O Lord, I believe").[160] As Archimandrite Robert Taft has shown, this prayer has been in use since at least the ninth century; and the Slavic use of it for the entire congregation, clergy and laity, goes back to the tenth century.[161] There

[158] Keleher, *Response to the Proposed Recasting of the Byzantine-Ruthenian Liturgy* (as in note 6 above), pp. 139-66. On the inserted phrase, see pp. 163-65.

[159] 2005 Great Friday Vespers, 7.

[160] 2005 Great Friday Vespers, 46-47.

[161] Robert F. Taft, "Prayers Before Communion in the Byzantine Eucharist," *Eastern Churches Journal* 8.1 (Spring 2001), 124-125, noting twenty-eight such prayers. For full discussion see his study, "Byzantine Communion Rites II: Later Formulas and Rubrics in the Ritual of Clergy Communion," *Orientalia Christiana Periodica* 68 (2002). See also Tkacz, "Singing Women's Words as Sacramental Mimesis" (as in note 86 above), 301-302, where its origins are shown to be the words of Martha, Peter, and Paul.

seems no merit to interrupting it now with so many blank lines.[162] At the very least, the two Trinitarian series of petitions beginning "Remember me" and "O God" could have been presented with no blank lines between. That is, each petition beginning "Remember me" could have begun flush left, so that the parallelism was clear:

> Remember me, O Lord, when You shall come into Your kingdom.
> Remember me, O Master, when You shall come into Your kingdom.
> Remember me, O Holy One, when You shall come into Your kingdom.

The new rubrics ("Also: ... Also: ...") suggest that the words are being laid out for textual analysis, not for prayer. In October of 2006 I saw briefly a more recent version of the proposed revised liturgy in use at SS. Cyril and Methodius Byzantine Catholic Seminary in Pittsburgh: In it the intrusive words were printed more faintly, but they were still present. [This remains the case in the revised *Divine Liturgy*.[163]]

It would be just as pedantic and inappropriate to interrupt the petition for travelers "by sea, air, and land." The historical facts that the original New Testament petition underlying this part of our liturgy referred only to sea and land and that the word "air" was added after the invention of aviation would not justify interrupting the flow of worship. To the contrary, respect for the prayer experience of the faithful should preclude inventing such rubrics. A finicky presentation of the petition for travelers "by sea, [Also: air,] and land" would be just as silly as the new rubrics "Also: ... Also: ...."

One new rubric is for the clergy: "Note that the celebrant only says all blessings."[164] Although several rubrics have been edited, this comment may be the solitary addition of its sort to the liturgy of March 25, 2005, and it is disconcerting that this simple comment is flawed, both grammatically and liturgically. First, the adverb is misplaced. As a result, grammatically this rubric means that the celebrant "only says" blessings. Presumably, however, the intention was to state that "only the celebrant" gives blessings. Liturgically, the word "says" is incorrect. The verb "says" is not synonymous with "gives." As the congregation asks during the dismissal, "Give the blessing." The celebrant's liturgical blessings involve him facing the people, moving his hand in the proper gesture, and chanting the words of blessing. None of this action is properly designated by the verb "say." It is even hard to imagine how an Eastern Catholic could have written the remark "the celebrant only says all blessings."

---

[162] Perhaps the line breaks are imitated from the *Divine Liturgy* books of 1978, but in those books the English and Slavonic are in parallel columns, and the narrowness of the columns forced the line breaks. In contrast, the layout for March 25, 2005, had no such constraint.

[163] See pp. 77-78.

[164] 2005 Great Friday Vespers, 26.

Translations

1. Biblical translations.

All the kinds of translation errors in the contemporary Roman Rite, errors which *Liturgiam Authenticam* seeks to correct, were introduced into the Ruthenian Rite on March 25, 2005. The poor English translation of the Psalms in use in the liturgies of that date is a reduction of psalmody into grade-school prose. Within Psalm 103, verse 4 is particularly curious, because the translation of just this verse seems to have been imported from the Douai translation of 1609 into a different translation of the Psalm as a whole. The verse on March 25, 2005, reads: "You make your spirits angels and your ministers a flaming fire." The first half is obscure and the second half sounds risky for the clergy. However, the root meaning of "angel" as "messenger" seems meant here, as it has been understood to be meant for ages. And "spirit" famously has many meanings, including "breath" or, as here, "wind." One has to reorder each pair of terms to make the meaning clear in English, because English is not nearly as inflected as Hebrew, Greek, Latin, or Slavonic: "You make the winds your messengers and flaming fires your attendants." That is clear, true, and poetic. That is the translation that has already been in use, for decades.

The Roman Rite in the past fifty years has been plagued by bad translations. Some of them "dumb down" the Bible and the liturgy, some ignore the traditional language of the Bible and the Fathers, and many obscure or down-play the Church's true theology. The ruling principle has been that the mass and the Bible should be easy to understand. Sadly the results are often banal and fall far short of the reality and mystery of God and of the Sacraments. Importantly, this means they also fall far short of the reality and mystery of human nature. The severity and pervasiveness of the problems made necessary the document described above, *Liturgiam authenticam.* The Eastern rites have hitherto been largely free of the problems of the Roman rite in this regard. The exception is that where the Eastern Rites now worship in English they have tended to use for lections the biblical translations that are popular with the Roman Rite.

2. Liturgical and hymn-text translations.

The translations of liturgical texts are likewise surprisingly oversimplified in the materials of March 25, 2005.[165] This is true of both the texts of the Divine Liturgy and also the texts of the hymnody. The prose style of the new translations favors simple statements. Subordination of clauses is avoided. Sentences are kept short. That is, the style has been dumbed down.

---

[165] On these translations, see also see Keleher, *Response to the Proposed Recasting of the Byzantine-Ruthenian Liturgy* (as in note 6 above), chapter ten, which discusses thirty-two questionable translations, some of which are also discussed in the present study.

Insofar as the Liturgy constitutes catechesis, it is catechesis for a lifetime, not just for eight-year-olds. Years ago when my husband was a boy worshiping with his grandparents at Holy Transfiguration Church in Fort William, Ontario, he called the feast of the Three Holy Hierarchs the feast of the "Three Holy Head Guys." That helped him to hold an initial idea of these saints, but it would have been woefully wrong if the Church had institutionalized a child's nomenclature. And, please note, it would have been a disservice to the child himself, because it would have falsely taught him that what he understood at first is All There Is. Moreover, in truth it is disrespectful to the child to treat a child's way of talking as liturgical norm: Children can experience mystery before they can articulate their experience. Downplaying mystery so that a child can understand all the words at a basic level at once, deprives the child of growing up in the presence of mystery.

a. **Theosis.** Sanctification is an important Catholic doctrine, well developed in the East. In the words of Cardinal Tomáš Špidlík, S.J., theosis, or theopoesis, "aims at bringing us into a living communion with Christ and with the Father, at 'deifying' us." Rooted in the Gospels and St. Paul, it was discussed by numerous Eastern Fathers including Gregory Nazianzus, Clement of Alexandria, Ignatius of Antioch, Athanasius, Maximus the Confessor, Symeon the New Theologian, and Gregory Palamas.[166] In the West, Latin discussions of the doctrine are also important, as in the writings of St. Thomas Aquinas. [167] In the past five centuries, the East has retained this teaching more effectively than the West. That is, through the liturgy, through its hymnody, through its prayers, the faithful are invited to seek the transforming, life-giving grace of God and to become holy. It is a matter of grave concern that the liturgy of 2005 vitiates much of this invitation by abandoning diction, by changing prayers, by muddying the structure and wording of hymns which for ten-to-fifteen centuries have served to draw the faithful into holy imitation (μίμησις, mimesis, in Cyril of Jerusalem).[168]

Some traditional theological language has been removed from the 2005 translation. To choose one of several possible examples, "pure" has been replaced by the word "clean."[169] This example is apt, for it involves a term resonant in Ruthenian tradition, in every liturgy, in the calendar (Pure Monday), as well as in the hymnody of March 25, 2005. Perhaps the reason for using "clean" instead of "pure" was to make the

---

[166] Tomáš Špidlík, S.J., now Cardinal, *The Spirituality of the Christian East*, Cistercian Publications 79 (Kalamazoo: Cistercian Publications, Inc., 1986), 45-51. For instance, see St. Athanasius, *De incarnatione* 54.3 (PG 25:192B).

[167] E.g., St. Thomas Aquinas, *Opuscula* 57:1-4.

[168] Discussed in Tkacz, "Singing Women's Words as Sacramental Mimesis," 275-276.

[169] For instance, in the Troparion of Great and Holy Friday, "The noble Joseph": 2005 Great Friday Vespers, 58. [See the revised *Divine Liturgy* , where it appears in the propers for the "Sunday of the Myrrh-Bearers," on p. 178.] For the word "pure" see above at pp. 20-21

texts understandable to children. (This, at any rate, was the rationale offered earlier via group email from the Metropolitan Cantor Institute for changing the name of the Feast of "The Encounter" to "The Meeting.")[170] The word "pure," however, is not a synonym for "clean." In Greek and in Slavonic, the words for pure resonate throughout. In our paschal katabasia Mary is "pure" (*čistaja*),[171] in the hymns of Joseph of Arimathea the linen used to wrap Christ's body is "pure" (*čistoju*),[172] and in every Divine Liturgy we thank God for having received the "most pure (*prečistych*)...Mysteries of Christ."[173] This language has to do with acknowledging the holiness of God, of the saints, and of the Sacraments. Further, the diction "pure" acknowledges that we are called to holiness. The language is a reminder of theosis. "Clean" rather suggests aspiring only to "I'm O.K., you're O.K."

Of course, some passages in fact use the biblical imagery of clean and unclean, which goes back to the Torah. Such is the Irmos of the Annunciation, "Let no unclean hand,"[174] discussed below.

b. Paradox. Our Christian mysteries contain paradoxes and ironies. That God became Man, that the Giver of Life died, and that by His death He conquered death, these are paradoxes to contemplate. The Incarnation and the Virgin birth are likewise mysterious. A hallmark of Byzantine sermons on, and meditations about, these doctrines is a direct statement of the paradox and often a thorough consideration of it, as, for instance, in several of the Holy Week hymns. In Greek and in Slavonic, these hymns often use word echo to emphasize the paradox and to honor the mystery. And the music has often drawn attention to these repeated words. Examples are "created...creation" in the first hymn of vespers, discussed below; "confined...is confined" (Slavonic *zatvorjajetsja...zatvorivyj*) and "creature... Creator" (*sozdanija... Sozdatel'*).[175] Sadly, the new translations of 2005 and also the musical settings of them fail to convey these characteristic liturgical techniques which are so distinctively Eastern.

c. Suppression of the masculine generic. A policy of suppressing the masculine generic is clearly at work in the revised Divine Liturgy. The word "man" is absent, often awkwardly replaced, the wording of the Beatitudes is revised, and the characteristic Eastern title for God as Lover of Mankind is altered.

---

[170] [The same change is found in the revised *Divine Liturgy* , e.g., on p. 321, "The Meeting."]

[171] 1976 Resurrection Matins, 29-31. See also, e.g., "all pure" on 10-11.

[172] *Solemn Vespers for Holy and Great Friday* (Pittsburgh: Byzantine Seminary Press, 1976), 38. Hereafter this will be cited as 1976 Great Friday Vespers.

[173] *Divine Liturgy* (1978), 27.

[174] *Divine Liturgy* (1978), 129. [See also the revised *Divine Liturgy* on p. 330.]

[175] 1976 Great Friday Vespers, 17-18.

i. *"Man."* The Creed itself is one of several parts of the Liturgy where the word "man" has been suppressed (detailed below), although the avoidance of the masculine generic is specifically prohibited by *Liturgiam Authenticam*.[176] The word "man" has been deleted from the prayer before the First Antiphon and from the prayer of offering voiced by the celebrant.

ii. *The Beatitudes*. Similarly, in the communion hymn based on the Beatitudes, the phrase "sons" of God (υἱοὶ, Matt. 5:9) has been changed to "children" of God.[177] This change ignores the dictional range of the New Testament: When "children" is meant, the word τεκνα is used, as in Rom. 9:7-8; when Mary finds her son in the Temple, she addresses the boy Jesus as Τέκνον (Luke 2:48).

More seriously, the whole thought-process behind changing the text of the Beatitudes requires comment. Changing "sons of men" to "children of God" is nothing less than correcting Jesus. Matthew was reporting Jesus' own words (in Greek, but then Aramaic also used the masculine generic). To change the words of Jesus implies a great deal about who Jesus is. If He was God Incarnate, He may be presumed to have had the ability to choose His words competently, at the very least. If Pentecost was real, then the Holy Spirit was active and able to insure that the Lord's words were competently recorded in the Gospels. If Jesus is God Incarnate, His words have an authority that must be respected.

iii. *"Lover of Mankind."* The words "man" and "mankind" are used in religious texts to mean the entire human race, past, present and future.[178] Identifying God as the "Lover of Mankind" reminds the faithful of being part of the communion of saints. One must be prayerfully careful when seeking to alter such expressions. "Lover of us all" is ambiguous, and it can mean simply "Lover of us persons in this room right now."[179] Given that the whole tenor of the revised liturgical texts seems to aim at reducing texts to what can be understood at first hearing, the phrase "lover of us all" will be taken in its simplest way.

Traditionally, in both theological and poetic language – and in the Divine Liturgy the language is often both theological and poetic – "God" is paired with "Man" or

---

[176] *Liturgiam Authenticam* (as in note 36 above), §§ 30-31.

[177] [See also the revised *Divine Liturgy* on p. 24.]

[178] See also Paul Mankowski, S.J., "The Necessary Failure of Inclusive-Language Translations: A Linguistic Elucidation," *The Thomist* 62 (1998): 445-68 at 462-63. Recently reprinted under the heading, "Jesus, Son of Humankind?" in *Touchstone*.

[179] [This politically change pervades the revised *Divine Liturgy* . For examples in the Divine Liturgy, see "God who loves us all" (p. 63) and "Christ … loves us all" (p. 90).]

"mankind," while "divinity" is paired with "humanity." The new version awkwardly pairs "God" with "humanity."

Moreover, as a New Feminist, one whose scholarship recovers authentic Christian traditions regarding women, I strongly advise against making such changes. Instead strengthen the presentation of the authentic doctrine that everyone, male and female, is called to holiness and that both male and female saints are models for everyone. What a loss it would be to abandon venerable, generic references to Mankind in favor of "Lover of humanity," to change the clear, powerful monosyllables of "God with man" into "God with humanity." As an Orthodox scholar observed, such modern revisions ultimately privilege ideology over the Incarnation.[180]

Shrunken lexicon and simplified syntax

Several words are absent from the liturgical materials of March 25, 2005, and the overall vocabulary used is smaller because variety has been reduced. For instance, "adore" is gone from the opening. The same overall simplification and homogenization has already occurred, of course, in English versions of the Roman Rite, with dreary results, and therefore *Liturgiam Authenticam* instructs that "a variety of vocabulary in the original text should give rise, insofar as possible, to a corresponding variety in the translations." Earnestly the Church wishes to avoid making holy worship appear to be "weakened or made trite" by reductionist translations. Examples are given:

> ...the use of a single vernacular term for rendering differing Latin terms such as *satiari, sumere, vegetari,* and *pasci,* on the one hand, or the nouns *caritas* and *dilectio* on the other; or the words *anima, animus, cor, mens,* and *spiritus,* to give some examples. Similarly, a deficiency in translating the varying forms of addressing God, such as *Domine, Deus, Omnipotens aeterne Deus, Pater;* and so forth, as well as the various words expressing supplication, may render the translation monotonous and obscure the rich and beautiful way in which the relationship between the faithful and God is expressed in the Latin text.[181]

The same principle applies when the original text is in Greek or Slavonic, as is seen in the examples below regarding the diction "beseech," "lifted," "long for." Several more changes of this sort are mentioned below, for instance, the substitution of "show" for "reveal." It is likely that idioms using "make" and "take" have greatly increased in the new liturgical materials, thus further reducing the variety of the original texts, and rendering them "weakened" or "trite."

---

[180] Kenneth Paul Wesche, "Man and Woman in Orthodox Tradition: The Mystery of Gender," *Saint Vladimir's Theological Quarterly* 37.2-3 (1993): 213-251, at 216-218.

[181] *Liturgiam Authenticam* § 51.

1. "Beseech"

In the liturgical materials of March 25, 2005, although the word "ask" was already in the ektenes (litanies), the same word "ask" was also substituted for "beseech." This is unfortunate, partly because the word "beseech" helps mark the difference between asking something from a fellow man and beseeching something from God. The verb "call out"[182] has also been replaced by "ask." Again *Liturgiam Authenticam* has a pertinent remark: "a deficiency in translating…the various words expressing supplication, may render the translation monotonous and obscure the rich and beautiful way in which the relationship between the faithful and God is expressed" in the original liturgical text.[183]

2. "For"

Substituting the word "because" for the word "For" is also unnecessary. Those of the faithful who do not know that "for" can be a conjunction can learn that from the context. "For" is preferable for the rhythm. Similarly, verb tenses have been needlessly recast into what was evidently deemed more familiar, as in the substitution of "will" for "shall" in the Beatitudes.[184]

3. "Alas!"

Often simple, mundane words are substituted for poetic language, and in some cases the change is not even to current idiom. "Alas…! Alas … !" is hardly contemporary, so it is unclear why it is preferable to the earlier expressions of "great sorrow."[185] "Woe is me" is the new substitution for "Great is my sorrow," a phrase of more dignity.[186] "Took" has replaced the clear and poetic term "lifted." "Count on" is the imprecise substitution for "long for."

4. "*A pure virgin*"

The Annunciation hymn used in 2005 recounts that the Archangel was sent to "a pure virgin."[187] That is a true statement. And it also is true that Greek and Slavonic are

---

[182] 1976 Great Friday Vespers, 5.

[183] *Liturgiam Authenticam* § 51.

[184] Discussed by Keleher, *Response to the Proposed Recasting of the Byzantine-Ruthenian Liturgy* (as in note 6 above), p. 203.

[185] 2005 Great Friday Vespers, 15-16; compare to 1976 Great Friday Vespers, 11-12.

[186] Compare 1976 Great Friday Vespers, 35, to 2005 version, 55.

[187] 2005 Great Friday Vespers, 17. [See also the revised *Divine Liturgy* on p. 325.]

not so obligingly clear with articles as is English, so that one could translate the hymn "a pure virgin." On the other hand, there is no compelling reason to change from the prior version's "the pure virgin" to "a pure virgin."[188] To the contrary, the pre-eminently pure virgin is the Theotokos, and she is unique, and may rightly be identified as "the pure virgin." Indeed, recalling the Slavic use of "pure" in an absolute sense when describing Mary, then the only "pure virgin" in this absolute sense is Mary, so that she alone can be called "the pure virgin."[189] In contrast, the phrase "a pure virgin" can be ambiguous, suggesting "one of many pure virgins." It is Orthodox and Catholic doctrine that Anne's conception of Mary was unique historically. Changing "the pure virgin" to "a pure virgin" does not seem well thought.

5. Christ's volition

An important Christian belief is that Christ fully willed His Passion. In the Divine Liturgy this is famously expressed in the anaphora when the celebrant recalls when Christ "was betrayed [παρεδίδοτο], or rather, when He handed himself over [παρεδίδου] ..." (italics mine). In English this must be expressed with different verbs, but in the original Greek the same verb, in the active voice, means "betrayed," but when it is reflexive and middle-voice it means "handed himself over."[190] In the proper hymns of Great and Holy Friday, the hymnode has used verbs in the same way. The old translation had the clause "when You placed Yourself for all mankind in a new tomb."[191] The new version has removed this reference to Christ's activity, even in His burial, by substituting the passive form "you were placed in a tomb" (italics mine).[192] While the difference may seem minor, the theological implications are real.

6. Absence of the word "orthodox"

Given that the word "Theotokos" has been added into the vocabulary in English of the liturgy, it would have been most appropriate to restore also the word "orthodox," a point made by Father Archimandrite Keleher.[193]

---

[188] There is variety, of course, in the translations used by (and within) the other Eastern Catholic rites and also the Orthodox Churches. One notes, though, that the Russian Orthodox Diocese of Alaska uses "the pure virgin" in a similar Marian proper hymn.

[189] See above at pages 20-21 and 50-51.

[190] Discussed in Tkacz, "Women as Types of Christ" (as in note 24 above), p. 300.

[191] 1976 Great and Holy Friday, 31.

[192] 2005 Great Friday Vespers, 52.

[193] Keleher, Response to the Proposed Recasting of the Byzantine-Ruthenian Liturgy (as in note 6 above), p. 269.

Literalism

Some changes come from intermittent literalism, while other changes are clearly quite different from the earlier English, as in the now-graphic description of the Virgin's grief.[194] The changes due to occasional literalism include the new omission of "be" from certain acclamations, substituting "wood" for "cross," etc. The literal translation of "salvation" has been promulgated where "safety and salvation" is both customary and, significantly, more accurate. That change is treated below in the discussion of the Prayers before the Lamp-Lighting Psalms.

1. To "be" or not to "be"

Dropping "be" from "Glory be to you, O God," is a case of literalism.[195] True, forms of "to be" can be omitted in statements in Greek, Latin, Hebrew, and many other languages, and in fact some liturgical phrases literally do not have a form of "to be" in the original language. That verb can be implied when it is not expressed. Thus for a translation to include the word "be" is not incorrect. Indeed, it makes better English than the omission. Moreover, familiar patterns, already memorized, are in use, some using "be" and others not, such as "Thanks be to God" and "Glory be to You, O Lord," but "Glory to God in the highest." It would be artificial to try to make these uniform. If the Slavonic were being translated into English for the first time, it might be a sound decision to mark the liturgical nature of the language by omitting "be." However, dropping "be" now introduces a repeated, distracting, minor, inessential change in long-accustomed practice, and it forces changing the way a great many passages in the liturgy are sung. This would seem to be tinkering.

It is, of course, fashionable among some contemporary Roman Catholics to jostle liturgical language in this way. But surely American fashions in the Roman Rite are not normative for the Eastern Catholic Churches. Moreover, one must set in context the recent removal of forms of the verb "to be" in the Roman Rite, as in the proclamation, "The Word of the Lord," after the Gospel is read. For decades the American English version of the Roman Rite has used language so mundane that the mass can be difficult to recognize as a liturgy. Arguably, the banality of the contemporary American liturgy then prompted another set of changes in language, such as taking out "to be," in an attempt to regain some sense of difference between liturgical language and ordinary speech.

Blessedly, the Ruthenian Rite has not been impoverished in this way and therefore there is no need artificially to remove forms of "to be" to show that it is liturgy.

---

[194] 2005 Great Friday Vespers, 15-16, compare to 1976 Great Friday Vespers, 11-12.

[195] [See also the revised *Divine Liturgy*, e.g. on p. 35.]

2. "Wood" / "Cross"

In the first hymn of Vespers, while the word "cross" is not in the Slavonic,[196] it was a reasonable way to handle the English translation. Although it is literally correct to use the word "wood,"[197] it is not clear that being literal here is useful. Many patristic and Byzantine texts use the word "wood" in contexts where modern custom uses "Cross." Sometimes a typological comparison is being made, for instance, between the wood of Isaac's sacrifice and the wood of Christ's Cross, or the wood of Noah's ark and the wood of the Cross. If, however, a direct typological comparison is not being made between two instances of "wood," then the word "Cross" is more readily understood. Not surprisingly, one parishioner, who was judging from the secularizing tendency of many of the changes throughout the revised liturgy, assumed that using "wood" here instead of "Cross" indicated a reluctance to name the Cross.

Inconsistency

No definite principles seem to inform the new translations. If simplicity is the guide, then why replace "priesthood" with "presbyterate"?[198] Why translate the single liturgical directive Ὀρθοί (*Orthoi*) in three ways?[199] Or φιλάνθρωπος (*philanthropos*) / φιλανθρωπία (*philanthropia*) in eight different ways?[200] Why retain the word "condescension"?[201] Indeed, that word is not only retained, it is given new emphasis by being shifted into final position, not just within the sentence, but in the entire hymn: "O Lover of humanity, glory to your condescension." It sounds quite Anglican. [Why omit the word "woman" where it had been customary but add it elsewhere (see p. 81 below)?]

Sadly, no Slavonic was included, even as an option.[202] No optional ektenes with the people's repeated prayer, *Hospodi, pomiluj* ("Lord, have mercy"). No *Otče naš* ("Our Father") in Slavonic, no occurrence of *Bohoróditsa*. The solitary exception was that several Slavonic musical terms were included in the 2005 materials: *samohlasen, bolhar, samopodoben, samopodoben: jehda ot dreva, samopodoben: So učeniki*. Retaining these

---

[196] 1976 Great Friday Vespers, 9-10.

[197] 2005 Great Friday Vespers, 14.

[198] 2005 Great Friday Vespers, 8.

[199] Keleher, *Response to the Proposed Recasting of the Byzantine-Ruthenian Liturgy* (as in note 6 above), p. 204.

[200] Keleher, op. cit., pp. 56-57.

[201] 2005 Great Friday Vespers, 51-52, 54.

[202] [This remains true in the revised *Divine Liturgy* .]

traditional designations is most welcome.[203] But excluding Slavic except for musical terms does rather suggest that musicology is more important, or more sophisticated, than anything else in the liturgy. By implication, Slavic was forbidden on March 25, because the materials expressly stated that no other text was to be used.[204] Is this not a voluntary Americanization? Or rather, an Americanization imposed by the hierarchy upon the clergy and the faithful.

Several specific passages

The myriad changes introduced into the revised Divine Liturgy cannot be treated exhaustively. Even the following representative sample of them is quite long. The character of the textual changes being made is shown by alterations in the diction of the prayers before the Lamp-Lighting Psalms; in the central Symbol of Faith (the Creed); in one of the most ancient hymns of eastern Christianity, "O Joyful Light; and in several other passages, including the Easter Troparion, the mystical priestly declaration *Sancta sanctis*, and the Irmos for the Annunciation. Musically, Psalm 140, the hymns of Vespers, and a variety of other chanted passages demonstrate what is being done to the music also. It is necessary to provide a detailed treatment of non-liturgical song, to show that modern, non-chant tunes are now being proposed as settings for liturgical texts, as if the modern tunes were liturgical chant.

1. Prayers before the Lamp-Lighting Psalms

The changes in the prayers before the lamp-lighting psalms are on the whole disappointing. [205] The exception is what seems to be a fine and reasonable change, from "priesthood" to "presbyterate." This change distinguishes the office itself from the holders of the office and makes the naming of this office parallel with naming the "diaconate." Other changes, however, obscure the theology.

---

[203] For the Slavonic musical terms, see 2005 Great Friday Vespers, 51 (*Samopodoben: Jehda ot dreva*) and 54 (*Samohlasen*); and 2005 Strasti -Matins for Great Friday (as in note 40 above), 5, 14, 15, 18 (*samohlasen*); 6 (*Bolhar*); 8, 10, 11, 12 (*samopodoben*); and 13 (*samopodoben: So učeniki*). [Slavic liturgical terms are retained in the revised *Divine Liturgy* . A virtue of that volume is that it explains them in the glossary at the end of the book.]

[204] "On and after the feast of the Holy and Pre-eminent apostles Peter and Paul, June 29, 2007, this text and its attendant music will be the sole liturgical text for the celebration of the Divine Liturgies of our Holy Fathers John Chrysostom and Basil the Great": revised *Divine Liturgy*, p. 3, the Foreword, signed by the four hierarchs, Most Reverend Basil M. Schott, O.F.M., Metropolitan of Pittsburgh; Most Reverend Andrew Pataki, Bishop of Passaic; Most Reverend William C. Skurla, Bishop of Van Nuys; and Most Reverend John M. Kudrick, Bishop of Parma.

[205] 2005 Great Friday Vespers, 8-10. Psalms 140, 141, 129 and 116 are the Lamp-Lighting Psalms.

a. The God-loving / God-beloved bishop.[206]Although the Greek is equivocal, with two possible meanings, the Slavonic translation of that Greek term is specifically one of those two possible meanings. A critical issue, then, is what importance lies in the Slavonic liturgy. That is, what authority is there in the Slavonic translation as witness to authentic tradition? Surely, the importance and authority are real.

In Greek the word is Θεοφιλεστάτου, and it can mean either "[most] God-loving" or "whom God loves [greatly]." [207] The Slavonic, however, is unambiguously "God-loving." The word is ъоҍолюъівім (bohol'ubiv'im). [208] The participle is from любіті (ljubiti, "to love"). [209] The Slavonic is the present active participle, dative plural: "God-loving."[210]Describing the bishop as "God-loving" is an affirmation of our belief in the apostolic succession. We, the faithful and the celebrant leading us, acknowledge the bishop to be our pastor, because the Holy Spirit has directed the authentic ordination and episcopal consecration of a man whose office holds him with a particular importance to the human vocation of loving God. God loves everyone, so there is no special reason to say that He loves the bishop. Frankly, the change rather suggests that the Metropolia is not going to commit itself to asserting that any given bishop loves God. But that kind of hedging of bets does not belong in the liturgy. We do not, after all sing "Maybe we praise you, maybe we bless you" or "Some of us praise you, some of us bless you." Liturgy is to transform the faithful through time into saints, and theosis is for bishops as well.

Seeking to elucidate the context for this term, I searched the term on the Thesaurus Linguae Graecae database.[211] Even limiting the search to the nominative and genitive singular retrieved 979 passages. Unfortunately, although the term is used frequently, its meaning is taken for granted and never explained. Nothing in any of the

---

[206] [In the 59-page analysis I gave to the hierarchs in April, 2005, this section was a single paragraph. Research with the Thesaurus Linguae Graecae in the fall of 2005 allowed me to expand the discussion to five paragraphs. The original point remains the same: the Slavonic tradition had "God-loving bishop," the Greek and Slavonic support that interpretation, and it is therefore the interpretation that the current Ruthenian rite should use. Happily, on this point the advice of the faithful in the Metropolia prevailed.]

[207] G. M. W. Lampe, *A Patristic Greek Lexicon*, 5 pts. in 2 vols. (Oxford: Clarendon Press, 1961-1968), s.v. Θεοφιλής, p. 642. Most modern translations of this Greek word omit the superlative, which I have therefore put in square brackets.

[208] *Divine Liturgy* (1978), 6, 14.

[209] Schmalstieg, *Old Church Slavic* (as in note 64 above), 133-136, 253. *Ljubiti* is, like *roditi*, of the first subcategory of fourth class verbs.

[210] Schmalstieg, *Old Church Slavic*, 134, 149-150.

[211] Consulted at the University of Notre Dame, October 28-29, 2005. The brief citations in the following notes are from the Thesaurus Linguae Graecae.

passages seems to suggest whether it is to be interpreted as "God-loving" or "God-beloved" or both ways at once, i.e., "God-loving-and-beloved." Basil of Caesarea (also called Basil the Great), Gregory Nazianzenos, and Anna Comnena are among those who use the term of bishops,[212] and the term is also used of bishops in the conciliar records from Ephesus (431).[213] The term has also been used to describe martyrs,[214] priests,[215] emperors,[216] archbishops,[217] metropolitans,[218] hegoumenoi,[219] synkelloi,[220] the chronicler Eusebius of Caesarea (a bishop),[221] and archdeacons.[222] It has also been applied to righteous persons of the Old Testament: Constantine VII Porphyrogenitos uses the term to describe Solomon[223]; the monk Georgios uses it of Moses[224]; Athansius I described King Hezekiah thus.[225] The term is found in conciliar documents, patriarchate

---

[212] Gregory Nazianzenos, *Epistula* 19, sect. 2, line 1; and *Epistula* 183, sect. 5, line 2; and *Epistula* 185, sect. 2, line 3 and sect. 5, line 4; Basil of Caesarea, *Letter* 32, sect. 1, line 1; also in *Letters* 52, 95, 99, 120, 127, 163, 181, 215, 217, 219, 223, 231; Anna Comnena, *Alexias*, Book 13, chapter 12, sect. 28, line 12.

[213] *Concilia Oecumenica, Conciliums universale Ephesenum anno 431* (Schwartz: *Acta conciliorum oecumenicorum*, vol. 1.1.1-1.1.7. The term is used of a bishop on Tome 1, vol. 1, pt. 1, pg. 94, line 5; 1.1.2, p. 22, line 4; 1.1.3, p. 8, line 4; etc. The term is also used of clerics of other ranks, e.g., in 1.1.2, p. 30, line 21; and 1.1.3, p. 66, line 10.

[214] E.g., Eusebius, *Historia Ecclesiastica* 5.21.4.1.

[215] E.g., Gennadius I, *De eis qui ad ecclesiam accedunt*, line 1: the priest Antonios; Georgius, *Vita sti. Theodori Syceotae*, sect. 124, line 2: the priest Demetrios; Theodoretus, *Letters, Collectio Patmensis*, Ep. 45, line 12: the priest Aetios.

[216] E.g., Eusebius, *Historia Ecclesiastica* 10.8.6.5; Athanasius, *De decretis Nicaenae synodi* 33.7.2 and 33.16.3; John Chrysostom, *Ad populum Antiochenum*, vol. 49, p. 220, line 23; Agathangelos, *Historia Armeniae*.

[217] E.g., Theodore the Studite, *Epistulae*, ep. 469, line 58: archbishop of Thessaloniki. Also ep. 511, line 63, ep. 522, line 61; Nicolaus I mysticus, *Ep.* 51, line 22.

[218] *Pochiron*, title 2, sect. 22, line 5; Nicolaus I mysticus, *Ep.* 181, line 1.

[219] E.g., Georgius, *Vita sti. Theodori Syceotae*, sect. 157, line 5.

[220] Constantine VII Porphyrogenitos, *De ceremoniis aulae Byzantinae*, p. 635, line 11.

[221] John Malalas, *Chronographia*, p. 228, line 19.

[222] Theodoretus, *Letters, Collectio Patmensis*, Ep. 14, line 2.

[223] Constantine VII Porphyrogenitos, *De virtutibus et vitiis*, vol. 1, p. 60, line 19.

[224] Georgius, monk, *Chronicon*, p. 117, line 21. "the great manifestor-of-God and God-loving Moses."

[225] Athanasius I, *Ep. 115 to Emperor Andronicus II* = ep. 41, line 3.

registers,[226] letters, chronicles,[227] hagiographic texts, including ones by S. John of Damascus,[228] and in monastic *acta*.[229]

Modern English translations of the term are important for attempting to determine its context and tradition. However, both "God-loving" and "God-beloved" are found. "God-loving" appears in various Orthodox, Catholic and Coptic websites, usually as part of the Divine Liturgy.[230] The designation "God-loving bishop" also recurs in English translations of hagiographic texts originally in Greek, Coptic and Russian. These English translations date between 1888[231] and 2004.[232] It is worth noting that a recent translation of "God-loving bishop" is by a scholar praised by Fr. Taft as having a "knowledge of Greek" that is "enviable."[233] One also finds the phrase "God-loving

---

[226] *Registrum Patriarchatus Constantinopolitani* (1315-1331), Doc. 10, line 17. The term is also in the registers for 1337-1350 and for 1350-1363, for instance.

[227] E.g., John Malalas, *Chronographia*, p. 228, line 19; Agathangelos, *Historia Armeniae*.

[228] E.g., Georgius, *Vita sti. Theodori Syceotae*, sect. 124, line 2; John of Damascus, *Passio magni martyris Artemii*, sect. 66, line 18; *Vitae et miracula scti Anasasii Persae*, sect. 2, line 10.

[229] E.g., *Acta Monasterii Pantocratoris*, ca. 1396, p. 161, line 7. The term is also used with "bishop" in monastic *acta* from the 11th -14th centuries from St. John Prodromos, Iviron, Esphigmenou, the Lavra, Xeropotamos, Chilandar, Patmos, and several others.

[230] The Divine Liturgy in English has "God-loving" in various online sources, including www.gis.net and web.ustpaul.uottawa.ca/Sheptytsky/... and www.antiochian.org/wordhtml/200411_20.html. It is also in an ektene in the ordination of a deacon: Saint Elias Church, Eparchy of Toronto (www.saintelias.com/ca/clergy/deacon.php). The following website is "dedicated to the God-loving Archpriest Victor Potapov": www.serfes.org/ missionary/january2004-april2004report.htm. The biography of Abba Mina concludes, "May the memory of this God-loving Bishop be eternal, Amen" (www.stmina-monastery.org/AbbaMina_the_Bishop_by_RamezRizkalla.pdf).

[231] *Theodoret's Letter to Leo* in Nicene and Post-Nicene Fathers, Series II, vol. 3, ed. Philip Shaff (New York: Christian Literature Publishing Company, 1892), 293. *The Martyrdom and Miracles of St. George of Cappadocia: The Coptic Texts edited with an English Translation*, ed. and trans. E. A. Wallis Budge (London, 1888), 253: People who had built a church dedicated to St. George "sent to Antioch and brought the God-loving Bishop, and he consecrated the church...." The Russian "Life of Metropolitan Peter" refers to the "God-loving bishop of Rostow, Simeon," at note 69 (www.cus.cam.ac.uk/~jrhll/petrmetpar.doc).

[232] "God-loving bishop Nonnos": translation of Heliodorus, *An Ethiopian Story* 8.9 (third or fourth century), in *Women's Religions in the Greco-Roman World: A Sourcebook*, ed. Ross Shephard Kraemer (Oxford: Oxford University Press, 2004), p. 383, using the translation of J. R. Morgan (1989): see p. 51. See also "Life of Matrona of Perge," trans. Jeffrey Featherstone, in *Holy Women of Byzantium: Ten Saints' Lives in English Translation*, ed. Alice-Mary Talbot (Washington, D.C.: Dumbarton Oaks Research Library and Collection, 1996), 44: "The blessed one...took counsel with them, that the sisters might go to the most God-loving bishop."

[233] Robert F. Taft, S.J., *A History of the Liturgy of St. John Chrysostom*, Vol. V: *The Precommunion Rites* (Rome: Pontificia Istituto Orientale, 2000), 40, writing of Jeffrey Featherstone, translator of the "Life of Matrona of Perge."

archbishop" in such translations.[234] The phrase "God-beloved bishop," however, is also found in some translations, from the Greek only.[235]

Given that the Greek is equivocal, that several scholars have interpreted the Greek exactly as the Slavonic does, and that the Slavonic rendering of the Greek is correct and unambiguous, surely the Ruthenian Church ought to rely on the Slavonic and translate the term as "God-loving." In addition, that is the way the term has customarily been translated throughout the Metropolia. [Happily, the Hierarchs did restore the phrase "God-loving Bishop" to the revised *Divine Liturgy*.[236]]

b. Final prayer. The final prayer of this revised ektene opens awkwardly and is devoid of the evocative language of "falling" and "lifting up," now replaced by references to "turning."

c. Tenth petition. Two passages in this ektene warrant special comments. The tenth petition, which had read, "for their safety and salvation," has become "for their salvation." Although this is literal and in a sense reasonable, the simplified translation neglects a difference between English and the prior liturgical languages involved, namely Slavonic and Greek. The Greek is σωτηρίας, which means both "safety" and "salvation." The corresponding word in Slavonic (*spasenij*) – as in Latin (*salvatio*) and other languages such as French (*salut*) – also carries both meanings. Modern English, however, has no single word which denotes both meanings. It was therefore a reasonable move of last century's translators to include both elements of the protection being sought in this petition, a protection comprised both of physical safety and spiritual salvation. In support of this point, one may note that Fr. Michael Gelsinger, Ph.D., a scholar with encyclopedic knowledge of Greek who was the founding chairman of the Department of Classics at the University of Buffalo, always used "safety and salvation" in this petition.[237] There is no need now to abandon that fullness. It is clear from context that translating the word as "safety and salvation" is appropriate, just as it is clear from the quite different context of the Symbol of Faith that translating the same word there as "salvation" is what the context requires: Christ became incarnate for us men and for our salvation; our physical safety did not require His Incarnation.

d. "Remembering…commend." More importantly, the prayer which formerly began "Remembering our most holy…" contains in the 2005 version two word-changes

[234] Zachariah of Mitylene, *Syriac Chronicle*, translated 1899, Book 5: "Timothy the revered and God-loving archbishop of the great city of Alexandria."

[235] Nicean and Post-Nicean Fathers, Series II, volume 7 (Gregory Nazianzenos, Letter 183), volume 8 (Basil's Letter 217), volume 14 (Pope Hadrian, Letters 16.6 on p. 538 and 10.15 on p. 224) and volume 38.

[236] [See revised *Divine Liturgy*, p. 12.]

[237] Rt. Rev. Serge Keleher, private communication.

that damage its theology. "Remembering" and "commemorating" are not synonyms, and neither are "commit" and "commend." The changes seriously change the meaning.

This petition is the culmination of the ektene: This final passage is far from being a different action, i.e., an act of personal commitment; rather it is another way of calling on the Lord to have mercy. That is why we are "remembering" (μνημονεύσαντες, *pomjanuvše*) our Lady and imitating her, which leads us to "commend (παραθώμεθα, *predadim*) ourselves and one another and our whole life to Christ our God." The verb for "remembering" is the same verb used in the various communion prayers which recall the words of the good thief, "Remember (Μνήσθητι, *Pomjani*) me, O Lord." No one would suggest altering that translation to "Commemorate me, O Lord." The conclusion of the ektene ought, it appears, to continue to be rendered as it has long been rendered, "Remembering our most holy...." Similarly, the opening of the ektene before the Our Father should begin "Now that we have remembered (*pomjanuvše*) all the Saints," rather than "...commemorated...."

The word "commend" in the ectenies retains its ancient meaning, important to Christians from the moment Jesus spoke it on the Cross: "Father, into Thy hands I commend (παρατίθεμα) my spirit" (Luke 23:45). Likewise, Paul and Barnabas "commended (παρέθεντο) to the Lord" the faithful in Lystra, Iconium and Antioch (Acts 14:23). The same verb is focal in the very Early Christian prayer the Commendation of the Soul, still used in the Roman Rite of Anointing.[238] That prayer is the commendation to God of someone who is ill, perhaps dying. The word "commend" was not casually chosen in that prayer or in the Divine Liturgy: Commending oneself to God is to act in imitation of Jesus.

Moreover, one can "commend" another person. But one cannot "make a commitment" for another person. The Eastern Rites have carefully preserved this distinction, which is crucial in the making of vows and affirmations of faith, as discussed immediately below. Thus it is proper and loving for the celebrant to ask the people to "commend... one another" to Christ. However, it is incorrect, even illogical, to ask the faithful to "commit... one another" to Christ, as the liturgy of March 25, 2005, had us do.[239] The changes in this direction to the people void its sense.

---

[238] For a full discussion of this ancient prayer and its Greek and Latin sources, see Chapter Three of Catherine Brown Tkacz, *The Key to the Brescia Casket: Typology and the Early Christian Imagination*, co-published in two series: Collection des Études Augustiniennes, Série "Antiquité", tome 165, and Christianity and Judaism in Antiquity Series, vol. 15 (Turnhout: Brepols, for the Institut d'Etudes Augustiniennes and University of Notre Dame Press, 2001).

[239] [See also the revised *Divine Liturgy*, e.g., on p. 13, 113.]

This text is particularly defining of our faith, and this makes the accuracy and soundness of its wording all the more important.

a. **"I believe."** It is a joy that our hierarchs have resisted Americanizing the opening of the Symbol of Faith.[240] Widespread among Roman Catholics of North America and Western Europe (but not in Africa or Poland or among Hispanics, for instance) is the practice of substituting "We believe...." for "I believe...," and *Liturgiam Authenticam* calls for the return to "I believe" in the Roman Rite, [a return that will occur in Advent, 2011].[241] Although using the plural pronoun "we" might seem to enhance the communal experience of the moment, the change is unwarranted, and in any case it often stems from a diminished theology.

Christianity traditionally honors the spiritual autonomy of the individual, that is, the ability and responsibility of the individual believer, male or female, to maintain orthodoxy. In the Gospels, only Peter, in the conversation in which Jesus declares him the rock on which He will found the Church, professes faith using the plural pronoun "we," speaking on behalf of the twelve (πεπιστεύκαμεν, John 6:70). When Martha professes her faith, she declares "I believe..." (ἐγὼ πεπίστευκα, John 11:27). The New Testament precedent is for the individual to profess faith as an individual. One may compare the profession of faith with the declarations made as part of the Holy Mysteries of Baptism and of Crowning in Marriage. Although several baptizands and/or their godparents/sponsors may make their professions in unison, each does so using the first-person singular, "I." Each person speaks individually to affirm renunciation of Satan, to attest commitment to Christ, to give witness personally to belief in Christ, to declare the Symbol of Faith, and to worship the Trinity. All these statements by the baptizands and godparents are voiced in the first person singular, "I do...," "I have...," "I commit myself to Him," and so on. Similarly, at a marriage crowning the bride and the groom each individually attests to having come freely and without reservation to the Mystery, answering the priest's interrogation in the first person singular, "I have." It would be insufficient for the two betrothed persons to speak in the plural: Each must speak as an individual, and neither has the authority to speak for the other. The same is true of the Symbol of Faith also. It is important to retain the original language's use of the first-person singular pronoun in order to express accurately what is occurring.

---

[240] [See also the revised *Divine Liturgy* on p. 1.]

[241] *Liturgiam Authenticam* (as in note 36 above) §§ 65 and 74, discussed by Serge Keleher, "*Liturgiam Authenticam*: Some Greek Catholic Comments," *Eastern Churches Journal* 8.1 (2001), 85-122 at 112-113; and Hitchcock, "New Era in the Renewal of the Liturgy" (as in note 116 above), 148; and Rev. Jerry Pokorsky, "*Liturgiam Authenticam* and the Prospects for Authentic Liturgical Renewal," in *Catholic Imagination*, 151-158 at 152. For the Nicene Creed in the Roman Missal, Third Edition, which comes into effect on the First Sunday of Advent, November 27, 2011, see http://www.usccb.org/romanmissal/samples-people.shtml.

The Symbol of Faith uses the first person singular, present indicative active: Πιστεύω. This is worth stating because there is a contemporary myth that the Nicene Council used the plural here. That myth was apparently invented to justify modern American usage of "We believe" as more authentic than any other practice. To the contrary, using the plural in the Creed seems to be entirely modern and in disregard of authentic Catholic and Orthodox tradition.

[Blessedly, the Roman Rite will restore the use of "I believe" to the Creed, beginning in Advent of 2011.]

b. **"Essence."** An excellent and deeply Eastern restoration in the revised liturgy is the correct translation of οὐσία (*ousia*) as "essence."[242] The Church Fathers deliberately used the philosophical term for "essence" to assert the Son's oneness of being with the Father. The revised translation of the Divine Liturgy restores the word "essence" (instead of "substance"). "Of one essence" (or "one in essence") is a more proper English rendering of the Greek word ὁμοούσιον (*homoousion*) used in the Creed itself and in early conciliar documents. The Latin rendering of οὐσία is *essentia*.

Such philosophically and theologically resonant diction is also found in the celebrant's reference to the λογικὴν λατρείαν (*logiken latreian*), which is well-translated as "rational worship." [243] The adjective λογικὴν appears to correlate with the word Λόγος (*Logos*) as used as a name for Jesus by St. John The Theologian in the opening verse of his Gospel: In the beginning was the Λόγος (John 1:1). Reason and contemplation are married in Christianity: "Rational worship" includes our rational awareness of our being grounded in the Logos; that is, it is rational to be aware of living in mystery. Sadly, the word "rational" has come into disfavor among some Eastern Christians in modernity, often through overemphasizing a contrast between the "spiritual" East and the "rational" West. After all, as just seen, the Greek Fathers who gave us the Creed used philosophical language such as οὐσία to express the reality of God's nature and being, for Christians to affirm and contemplate. It is unfortunate that the provisional version of the Divine Liturgy renders the phrase λογικὴν λατρείαν (*logiken latreian*) as "spiritual sacrifice."[244]

c. **"Men" and "Son of Man."** The creedal affirmation that Jesus Christ acted "for us men" ought to be honored and that translation ought to be retained in English. Moreover, the creedal phrase "for us men" has linguistic affinities with the Gospel phrase "Son of Man," which Our Lord transformed into a title for himself, and also with the

---

[242] [See also the revised *Divine Liturgy* on p. 51.]

[243] *The Sacred and Divine Liturgy of our Holy Father John Chrysostom* (Toronto: Basilian Press, 1988), 109, 113: Keleher, *Response to the Proposed Recasting of the Byzantine-Ruthenian Liturgy* (as in note 6 above), 184.

[244] Keleher, op. cit., 184.

Creation of "man" recounted in Genesis. Any English translation of the Symbolum, therefore, ought to convey these associations through retaining the word "men." Instead, the revised form of the Creed introduces a deeply regrettable change and reads "for us and for our salvation."[245]

i. The "Son of Man," the Book of Daniel, and the Gospels. The prophet Daniel recounted visions of Christ, His death, the destruction of Jerusalem, and the coming in the clouds of the "son of man" to the throne of the "Ancient of Days," an event issuing in the eternal kingdom of the saints. The unique Aramaic phrase *k'bar ĕnāš* (found only in Daniel 7:13) was translated by Jews in both the Septuagint and Theodotion-Daniel as υἱὸν ἀνθρώπου "son of man," and the same Greek diction is found in the Gospels in reports that Jesus prophesied, "And you will see the son of man coming in the clouds of heaven" (Matt. 24:30, 26:64; Mark 14:62; Luke 21:27). Moreover, in the Gospels the phrase, used some seventy times, is given emphasis by the addition of definite articles: τὸν υἱὸν τοῦ ἀνθρώπου. As Raymond E. Brown and others have noted, the articles add emphasis and thereby elevate the phrase into virtually a title.[246] Thus did Jesus overtly identify himself as the subject of Daniel's first vision.

Some scholars, including Brown, affirm that Jesus' use of the words from Daniel is deliberate. For instance, William Barclay holds that Jesus "quoted Daniel 7:13 with its vivid account of the ultimate triumph and kingship of God's chosen one [Matt. 26:64]. He well knew what he was doing."[247] At present, however, most academics take great pains to assert that Jesus did not use the phrase; instead, they aver, the Evangelists merely put the words into His mouth. Basic to that view is the contention that in the Old Testament the phrase must refer to (and only to) the Jews who suffered under the persecution of Antiochus IV.

A corollary to this contention is the idea that the Book of Daniel is a literary fiction composed during the time of the persecution by Antiochus IV in the second century B.C., not a prophet book composed centuries earlier.[248] By this view, there is no prophecy in Daniel's vision. Moreover, the Pharisees during the Christian Era asserted that prophecy

---

[245] [This change is also in the revised *Divine Liturgy* on p. 51.]

[246] Raymond E. Brown, S.S., *Death of the Messiah: From Gethsemane to the Grave: A Commentary on the Passion Narratives in the Four Gospels*, 2 vols. (New York 1994), 1:507.

[247] William Barclay, *The Gospel of Matthew*, 2 vols., rev. ed. (Philadelphia, 1975), 2:355. For an eloquent and full defense of Jesus' use of the phrase, see Chrys C. Caragounis, *The Son of Man: Vision and Interpretation* (Tübingen: J. C. B. Mohr [Paul Siebeck], 1986).

[248] Bruce D. Chilton, *Four Gospels 1992* (Louvain: Peeters, 1992), 203 and 218; Di Lella, *Book of Daniel* (as in note 20 above), 92, 97, 206, 219; with n. 234 citing sixteen other concurring scholars from 1900 to 1977. A particularly vehement and badly reasoned case for this view is Maurice Casey, *Son of Man: The Interpretation of Daniel 7* (London: SPCK, 1979), 25, 27, 39, etc.

ended with Ezra, Nehemiah, Haggai, Zechariah, and Malachi: "With these writers, the Scriptures inspired by God's Spirit came to an end."[249] By that pharisaic interpretation, the whole book of Daniel, when dated to the second century B.C., is placed after the age of prophecy. Obviously Jesus himself was born after the putative end of prophesy, so that the pharisaic interpretation implies that his prophecies are not valid. An effect, if not indeed the intention, of that pharisaic pronouncement (that prophecy had ended) is to downplay and even to attempt to invalidate certain scriptures and interpretations that Christians, and indeed Christ himself, have relied upon.

Implied in the current majority view is the unacceptable idea that the Septuagint translation and Theodotion-Daniel are valueless: Some scholars state that the Greek Scriptures translate the phrase "Son of Man" as it "should not" be rendered.[250] Moreover, these writers implicitly hold that Jesus and the Evangelists were wrong to quote the Greek translations made by Jews. Summarizing and countering this trend, Raymond E. Brown states:

> The debate whether historical Jesus used this title [i.e., Son of Man] of himself or whether it is a product of early christian reflection retrojected into Jesus' ministry has raged throughout the last hundred years. If one takes the latter view, one faces two major difficulties: Why was this title so massively retrojected, being placed on Jesus' lips on a scale far outdistancing the retrojection of "the Messiah," "the Son of God," and "the Lord"? And if this title was first fashioned by the early church, why has it left almost no traces in non-Gospel NT literature, something not true of the other titles?[251]

ii. The "Son of Man" and the Creed. The Council Fathers certainly accepted the validity of the Gospels and they accordingly understood "Son of Man" as a title the Lord chose to refer to himself. As a result, we today may take seriously the linguistic parallels between the phrases "Son of Man" in the Gospels and "for us men" in the Symbolum. The Greek of the Creed clearly has "for us men": δι' ἡμᾶς τοὺς ἀνθρώπους. Moreover, in this phrase the Fathers of the Council of Nicaea (325) included the article τοὺς before the noun ἀνθρώπους ("man"), which gives added emphasis to the word in precisely the way the article gives emphasis to the word "man" in the phrase "Son of Man," τὸν υἱὸν τοῦ ἀνθρώπου.

iii. "Man," Creation, and the Creed. In the Greek Scriptures, the word "man" (ἄνθρωπος) is focal in the Creation account, where it is used generically in the revelation

---

[249] Hengel, *Septuagint as Christian Scripture* (as in note 15 above), 45.

[250] An instance of a scholar asserting how the text "should not" be rendered is Di Lella, *Book of Daniel*, 87. Although he treats only Aramaic and English, his comments also apply to the Greek.

[251] Brown, *Death of the Messiah*, 1:507, see also 2:1478-79, 1481.

that God created man, male and female (Gen. 1:26, 27). In the Creed the emphasized word "men" aligns Creation, Incarnation, and the purpose of the Incarnation. Deleting "men" is a bow to political correctness and would result in a Liturgy with a limited shelf-date.

3. O Joyful Light

The oldest non-Scriptural hymn in Christian use, known in many of the Western Churches as well as in the East, *Phos Hilaron* (φῶς ἱλαρόν) "is a praise of the Trinity for Christ, true 'light of the world' (Jn. 1:9) of which the evening lamp was a symbol."[252] This contemplative hymn is far better poetically and musically in the earlier English version than in that of 2005. The verbal changes introduced in 2005 are pedantic and literal; passages with differences are italicized in both English versions below. The musical changes seem motivated by an inappropriate desire to make the song different. None of these changes seem necessary or even well-thought. [The 2005 version was promulgated in the revised Divine Liturgy.]

> **Slavonic:** Sv'ite tichij, svjatyja slavy, bezsmertnaho Otca nebesnaho, syjataho blažennaho, Isuse Chiste, prišedše solnca na zapad, vid'ivše svit večernij, pojem Otca i Syna i Svyataho Ducha Boha. Dostojin jesi vo vsja vremena p'it byti hlasy prepodobnymi, Syne Božij, život dajaj vsemu miru, jehože radi ves' mir slavit t'a.[253]

> **Prior English:** O Joyful Light! *Light and* Holy Glory of the Father immortal, the Heavenly, Holy, *the Blessed* One; O Jesus Christ. Now that we have reached the setting of the sun and see the evening light, we sing to God, Father, Son, and Holy Spirit. It is fitting at all times to raise a song of praise in measured melody to You, O Son of God, the Giver of Life. *Behold*, the universe sings Your glory.[254]

> **2005 English:** O Joyful Light *of the Holy* Glory of the Father Immortal, the heavenly, holy, *blessed* One; O Jesus Christ! Now that we have reached the setting of the sun and see the evening light, we sing to God, Father, Son, and Holy Spirit. It is fitting at all times to raise a song

---

[252] Robert F. Taft, ""Phos Hilaron," *ODB* (as in note 47 above), s.v.

[253] 1976 Great Friday Vespers, 19. In the present study, the variant reading of the Church Slavonic is not addressed, but obviously for a full consideration of the song, it should be.

[254] 1976 Great Friday Vespers, 19-20.

of praise in measured melody to You, O Son of God, the Giver of Life. *Therefore* the universe sings Your glory.[255]

In the first line of this hymn, the earlier translation repeats the word "light" for the sake of the poetry, both the sound and meaning of the word. Also, the second iteration of "light" receives the musical emphasis of the second musical phrase. In the new version, that emphasis is given to the word "of" and the word that is repeated in the first sentence is not "light" but, again, "of." In the Slavonic Rite, indeed in Catholicism, fullness of meaning is supposed to trump literalism.

As for the word "the" before "blessed one" in the earlier version, one must note that the Slavonic and Greek of this hymn lack the grammatical article ("the") entirely, which is usual in those languages. English adds the article for clarity and grace of expression, and evidently the prior English translation had added the word "the" to fit the words well to the music. In the prior English version the presence of the unemphasized word "the," which is sung on a lower pitch than the following word "blessed," produces a natural emphasis on the word "blessed."

Musically, the changes are as petty and ineffective as the verbal ones. Consider the altered notes for the phrase "measured melody to You." A frequent trait of the new settings is seen here, namely, a rather mechanical musical movement. The change introduced here makes the passage perfunctory, where it was graceful before. In both the prior and the 2005 versions, "measured melody to You" concludes the third of a set of sentences, each having the same general melodic line. In the prior version, the first two sentences end with a phrase consisting of a quarter note (F) leading to a tranquil set of descending half notes (G, F, E) with the words "evening light" and "Spi-i-rit." Then, in pleasing variation, the third line, the final one of the series, slightly changes the timing: after the quarter note (F) follow dotted half, quarter, dotted half (G, F, E). This musical change fitly prepares for the direct address to the Son of God which concludes the hymn. The 2005 version is different. In it, each of the three sentences ends with two beats on G, two on F, and two on E, so nothing marks the third sentence as the final one leading to the address to God.

The last line of the 2005 hymn lacks the wondrous resolution of the earlier version. The word "Behold!" is an ancient and liturgically sound way of calling attention to a wondrous sight, and the entire hymn is about Light. The hymn is to Jesus Christ, Joyful light of the Father. The sun has set, and the "evening light" is visible, and again we sing to God. The hymn culminates with our singing to the Light Himself, "Behold! the universe sings your glory." This is a heavenly hymn. The theology, the poetry are heavenly, and the music should be too. Inanely, the word "Therefore" has been substituted for "Behold." Literally, that is correct: In fact, the opening of the final line of

---

[255] 2005 Great Friday Vespers, 22. [In the revised *Divine Liturgy* , see p. 117.]

text, *jehože radi*, literally means "for the sake of this."[256] The poetic problem is that evidently no way exists to express this logical transition that also deserves to be the musical highpoint of the hymn. "Therefore" is less bad than "For this" or "And so," of course. On the other hand, "Behold" fits poetically and the logical connection is conveyed implicitly. The rhythm of the prior musical version builds effectively to the final words, "your glory." In the 2005 version the word "universe" has more emphasis.

4. First hymn of vespers, Great and Holy Friday

The prior version had theologically inspired word echo on "creation ... created": "All creation suffered with the One Who created all things."[257] Moreover, the musical setting had emphasized the echoed words: the accented syllable of "creation" and of "created" is in each case a dotted half note on a B. Musically, attention was put where the text puts attention. "Things" is the repeated word in the 2005 version of this hymn: "All things suffered along with you, who made all things."[258] (Adding "along" is another poor change.) The last sentence, too, is less effective than the 1976 version.

In Slavonic chant, as also in Gregorian chant, often the musical line echoes the meaning of the words.[259] This is true in the next stichera for Great and Holy Friday. In the 1976 version, the music rose with the words "raised upon the cross."[260] Unfortunately, in the 2005 words, the music descends with the words "lifted up on the wood."[261]

One addition in the 2005 version is unintelligible. In the original poem, Jesus is presented as reviewing His good deeds in imagined address to His condemners. The 1976 version begins: "O, how could the lawless council condemn to death the King of Creation without being ashamed at the thought of His good works which He recounted

---

[256] *Radi*: "for, for the sake of, postposition requiring genitive case"; and *jegože*: relative pronoun, genitive singular masculine; Schmalstieg, *Old Church Slavic* (as in note 64 above), 65 and 272.

[257] 1976 Great Friday Vespers, 9.

[258] 2005 Great Friday Vespers, 13.

[259] For this in Gregorian chant, see Tkacz, "Singing Women's Words as Sacramental Mimesis" (as in note 86 above), e.g., at 313-314.

[260] 1976 Great Friday Vespers, 10.

[261] 2005 Great Friday Vespers, 14.

to them saying…"[262] The 2005 text obscurely states: "They felt no shame when he recalled his good deeds which he had foreshadowed when he said to them…"[263]

5. *The prokimenon of Great and Holy Friday*

A prokimenon is a psalm verse chanted before the epistle during the Divine Liturgy. The text was presented in a poor translation on March 25, 2005.[264] The old translation had a strong text, and the old music aptly emphasized the words "pit" and "death":

> **R:** You have plunged me into the bottom of the pit, into the darkness and the shadow of death, into the darkness and the shadow of death. **V:** O Lord, God of my salvation, by day and by night I cry out to you.[265]

Oddly, the new translation seems to avoid the word "death" and repeats "depths…depths…depths."

> You have laid me in the depths, in the depths of the tomb,
> in places that are dark, in the depths. [no verse][266]

One need only utter the word "depths" aloud to realize the awkwardness of singing it three times. The words "pit" and "death" are more readily pronounced. The prior translation was better, and by far more singable.

6. *Welcome / receive*

In the second part of the Cherubic Hymn (or Cherubikon) one word is changed: "receive" is substituted for "welcome" ("That we may receive the King of all").[267] The Greek is ὑποδεξόμενοι and means "receive," including "receive as a guest," and so it

---

[262] 1976 Great Friday Vespers, 15-16.

[263] 2005 Great Friday Vespers, 19.

[264] 2005 Great Friday Vespers, 26.

[265] 1976 Great Friday Vespers, 23.

[266] 2005 Great Friday Vespers and Liturgy, 23.

[267] [See also the revised *Divine Liturgy* on p. 42.]

also means "welcome."[268] Either word, "welcome" or "receive," is correct, and each has nuances that are appropriate. Either verb readily allows the faithful to think of mystical meanings, that is, of receiving and welcoming the Lord in the Eucharist. Although in English, using "receive" creates a verbal parallel with the English of the Roman mass, in the use of the Centurion's words, "Lord, I am not worthy to receive you," the parallel is only in English, for the Greek for the Centurion's word is not ὑποδέξομαι. The reason for the proposed substitution is not clear. There could be a valid reason, or it could be mere tinkering.

7. The Easter troparion

Similar are the substitutions in the Easter troparion. Although this of course was not part of the materials of March 25, 2005, but has appeared since, this text has such prominence in worship that it warrants mention here. The pertinent words are italicized below for ease of comparison. The prior text was:

> Christ is risen from the dead! By death he *conquered* death
> and to those in the *graves* he granted life!

The new translation is as follows:

> Christ is risen from the dead! By death he *trampled* death
> and to those in the *tombs* he granted life![269]

The changes are "conquered" to "trampled" and "graves" to "tombs." Related is the Hymn of the Incarnation, with its praise of God, for "By death you conquered/trampled death." Both "conquered" and "trampled" are correct renderings of the underlying Greek, πατήσας (Slavonic *popravyj*): Its sense is "to tread on, to trample," and so, metaphorically, "to defeat utterly, to conquer." Perhaps there is an intention behind the revised translation, to reserve "conquer" for translating a different verb, νικάω. If so, then "trampled" may be the better choice here. A great deal rests on how the two Greek terms are used in the Bible, and how the Slavonic terms are used in Slavonic Scripture:

---

[268] See, e.g., Barclay M. Newman, Jr., *A Concise Greek-English Dictionary of the New Testament* (London: United Bible Societies, 1971), reprinted at the back of *The Greek New Testament*, 3rd ed., ed. Kurt Aland, Matthew Black, Carlo M. Martini, Bruce M. Metzger, and Allen Wiggren, in cooperation with the Institute for New Testament Textual Research (Münster/Westphalia: United Bible Societies, 1975).

[269] [This translation is used in the revised *Divine Liturgy* , e.g. on p. 164.]

popirati is used in the Parable of the Sower (Luke 8:5), but without evident pertinence to the Paschal Troparion.[270]

As for "tombs," if one is aiming for ready understanding, "graves" would win over "tombs." However, if "trampled" is the better choice in this sentence, then the alliterating "tombs" is a plausible companion. Even so, "graves" and "granted" make a stronger alliterative pair, and they are closer together within the sentence than are the two words "trampled" and "tombs." The earlier English had strong alliteration: "conquered...graves...granted," and this alliteration is augmented by the presence of -r- in each of these words. The prior version is, in its sounds, more emphatic. And it has been sung by heart for decades.

8. "Testament" or "Covenant"?

For Greek Christians in particular, the language of "testament" and "covenant" is of interest, because it was the Greek of the Septuagint that introduced the two terms into Scripture and thence into the liturgy. The proposed change from "testament" to "covenant" in the anaphora seems entirely appropriate both because it is consonant with the Greek Scriptures and also because it is in accord with the symbolism of the architecture of all Catholic churches, and in particular with that of Eastern churches.

In Hebrew, a single word, *berith* (lit. "binding"), indicated an agreement, whether between equals (as when Jacob and Laban made compact, Gen. 31:44, 47), or between God and man (as in Gen. 15:18). For the latter circumstance, the pre-Christian Jews who translated the Torah into Greek borrowed the Greek term for "will" (as in "last will and testament"), because in a sense the testator, being the one to bequeath something, was in the superior position, as God is profoundly in the superior position in the covenant with mankind. The Septuagint uses διαθήκη (*diatheke*) for God's covenant and συνθήκη (*syntheke*) for human contracts.[271] Thus the word διαθήκη is used in the Septuagint for the making of the covenant with Abraham and his heirs (Gen. 17:1-19). In Exodus, when God had confirmed His covenant with the people, Moses sprinkled some of the blood of the peace offerings upon the people and proclaimed, "Behold the blood of the covenant [διαθήκη], which the Lord hath made with you concerning all these words" (Exod. 24:8). The Decalogue is the "tables of the covenant [διαθήκη]" (Num. 10:33). Jeremiah prophesies of a "new covenant" (διαθήκην καινήν) to be written on the heart (Jer. 38 [MT 31]:31-34). Isaiah foretells of God's servant, often referring to the covenant (Isa.

---

[270] Schmalstieg, *Old Church Slavic* (as in note 64 above), 201.

[271] See *The Westminster Study Edition of the Holy Bible* (Philadelphia: The Westminster Press, 1948), 95 of the "Concordance...with Definitions...," s.v. "Testament." The main sense of συνθήκη is "a composition of words and sentences" and the extended sense is "contract, covenant": Liddell and Scott, *Intermediate Greek-English Lexicon* (as in note 57 above), s.v.

42:1-4, 49:1-6, 50:4-9, 52:13-53:12). Indeed, this servant is not only entrusted with the covenant (διαθήκη; Isa. 42:6): He embodies it (διαθήκη; 49:8).

The influence of the Greek of the Septuagint upon developing Christian thought is seen in regard to this term in the Epistle to the Hebrews. The fact that the original Hebrew word when used to mean "covenant with God" had been translated by a Greek word that meant "will, testament" (διαθήκη) led to meditation upon the implications of this.[272] This is very much to the fore in Hebrews 9:15-17, where the death of the testator is cited as essential in order for the heirs to receive their inheritance.

Jesus stated at the Last Supper that the chalice held "my blood, of the Διαθήκης" (Matt. 26:28, see also Mark 14:24, Luke 22:20). All manuscripts have the word Διαθήκης. Some early witnesses include the word Καινῆς ("New"); these include the Byzantine lectionary as well as Coptic, Ethiopian, Georgian, and Armenian sources. Irenaeus, Origen, Cyprian, Basil and Chrysostom also include "New."[273] The Vulgate rendered this as "novi testamenti." The Letter to the Hebrews echoes Jesus' reference to His blood (αἵματι Διαθήκης, haimati Diathekes), augmenting the Lord's words by describing the Διαθήκης as αἰωνίου (aioniou, "eternal," Heb. 13:20).

The two parts of Scriptures, the revelation to the Jews and the revelation through Christ, are known as the Old Testament and the New Testament. The history of that familiar terminology may well be pertinent to the anaphoral quotation of Our Lord's words and should probably be considered in deciding how to render Διαθήκης into English. Ideally, the Eastern Churches in the English-speaking parts of the world would have an orthodox translation of the Septuagint and New Testament for liturgical use, and the word used to translate διαθήκη in the Old Testament should be used to translate Jesus' words at the Last Supper, both in the Gospels and in the anaphora. Further, the pertinent passages should also be studied in the Slavonic translation of the Bible, when determining how to render the words of the anaphora into English.

In the Greek of the Divine Liturgy, the anaphoral statement refers to τὸ Αἷμά μου, τὸ τῆς Καινῆς Διαθήκης. In the English translation of the Divine Liturgy in use for several decades, the anaphoral wording was, this is "my blood of the new testament."[274] In the proposed new English version, "Testament" has become "Covenant." Recently the Roman Mass has adopted the word "Covenant" in the words

---

[272] The primary meaning of διαθήκη, attested in Aristophanes, et al., is "a disposition of property by will, a will, testament" and a secondary meaning, attested in the New Testament, was "an arrangement between two parties, covenant": Liddell and Scott, *Intermediate Greek-English Lexicon*, s.v.

[273] See apparatus of *The Greek New Testament* for both Gospel passages.

[274] See, for instance, *The Divine Liturgy of Our Father Saint John Chrysostom*, adapted from tradition[al] chants for congregational use by the Inter-Eparchial Music Commissions of Pittsburgh and Passaic, published with ecclesiastical approbation (Pittsburgh: Byzantine Seminary Press, 1965, 10ᵗʰ reprint 1997), 22.

of institution. There certainly seem to be strong grounds for the use of "Covenant" here by the Ruthenian Rite as well.

A further area of significance in translating these words is that the Eastern Churches have maintained more closely than the contemporary Roman Church the architectural correlation of the Christian sanctuary with the Holy of Holies in the Temple, where formerly the Ark of the Covenant resided. In the synagogue, the Torah niche recalled the placement spatially. When the Ark had been lost and the Holy of Holies emptied, synagogues were aligned in the direction of Jerusalem so that when the congregation faced the Torah they also faced Jerusalem, site where formerly the Ark had resided. As our Holy Father Benedict XVI observed in 2000:

> In the synagogue the worshippers looked beyond the "Ark of the Covenant," the shrine of the Word, toward Jerusalem. Now, with the Christian altar, comes a new focal point. Let us say it again: on the altar, what the Temple had in the past foreshadowed is now present in a new way.[275]

This recognition is evident in even the earliest description of the structure of a Christian church, from 318, in Greek, for it calls the altar "the holy of holies."[276] More precisely, Eusebius of Caesarea redefines the holy of holies as the altar.[277] This is a deliberate and emphasized comparison of the new church building with the prior Temple and of the New Sacrifice of the Eucharist with the repeated Temple sacrifices. Eusebius demonstrates the active awareness Christians had of the parallel between the Temple and the church, both in liturgy and also in architecture. Even in this Greek writer we find Christianity "speaking and thinking in a Semitic way."[278] The Divine Liturgy is consonant with this use of Semitic, profoundly Jewish terminology in referring to the eucharistic altar, and the word for "Covenant" is important in this context. Thus it appears that to revise the English translation of the words of the anaphora from "testament" to "Covenant" befits Christian tradition, and it particularly suits the tradition of Eastern Christianity. [The revised Divine Liturgy does use the word "Covenant" here.]

---

[275] Ratzinger, now Pope Benedict XVI, *Spirit of the Liturgy* (as in note 89 above), 70-71.

[276] τὸ τῶν ἁγίων ἅγιον θυσιαστήριον: Eusebius of Caesarea, *Ecclesiastical History* 10.4.44. For the Greek, see Eusèbe de Césarée, *Histoire Ecclésiastique*, 4 vols., ed. Gustave Bardy, Sources Chrétiennes 41, 55, 73 (Paris, Éditions du Cerf, 1952, 1955, 1958, 1960). Book 10 is in volume 3. Although in English the word "altar" interrupts the phrase "holy of holies," in Greek the word for "altar" is at the end of the phrase.

[277] Thus Roy J. Deferrari translates the phrase as "the holy of holies, the altar," following the Greek word order and conveying the meaning exactly: *Ecclesiastical History*, trans. Roy J. Deferrari, 2 vols., Fathers of the Church vols. 19 + 29 (New York: Fathers of the Church, Inc., 1953, 1955), 2:259.

[278] Ratzinger, now Pope Benedict XVI, *Spirit of the Liturgy*, 75. His comment, which was made more generally about the early Church, aptly describes Eusebius' use of the language of "holy of holies."

One hopes that there will be sermons preached on the physical reality of the sanctuary, with the new Holy of Holies being the locus of the real presence of God in the blood of the New Covenant, surpassing even the wondrous presence of God in the original Holy of Holies, which contained the Ark of the original Covenant.

9. *"Holy for the holy"/"Holy gifts to holy people"*

Immediately after the Lord's Prayer and just before the reception of the Eucharist, together the celebrant and the congregation voice a modified echo of the threefold angelic cry of "Holy." As Rev. Archimandrite Fr. Taft has shown, it has been a part of the Divine Liturgy "throughout the Christian East" since at least the fourth century.[279] The "holy things" are possible because the Holy One made them so, for the sake of the holy, i.e., the baptized who seek healing and sanctification through the Eucharist. The three iterations of "holy" are divided between the celebrant's declaration and the congregation's following hymn. The first "holy" refers to the holy Eucharist, the second "holy" refers to the faithful who are about to receive it, and the third "holy" opens the congregation's meditational hymn praising the mystery of the One Holy Lord, Jesus Christ. The earliest commentaries on this passage identified the saints as the baptized, following the usage in the New Testament.[280]

The celebrant's liturgical call is expressive of theosis, as was explained by Nicholas Cabasilas (1319/23, † before 1391):

> Those whom the priest calls holy are not only those who have attained perfection but those also who are striving for it without having yet obtained it. Nothing prevents them from being sanctified by partaking of the holy Mysteries, and from this point of view being saints.... [The people respond, "One is holy,"] for no one has holiness of himself;...Christ...the only Holy One pours himself forth upon the faithful.[281]

Similarly Symeon of Thessalonika (d. 1429) "interprets the Sancta sanctis as a Christological confession like Philippians 2:11, a proclamation that we are one in the

---

[279] Taft, "Holy Things for the Saints" (as in note 21 above), 87-88. See also Taft, *Precommunion Rites* (as in note 230 above), 230-248, at 234 and 240.

[280] Taft, "Holy Things for the Saints," 89, with note 25 on p. 99 citing Acts 9:13, 32; Rom. 1:7, 8:27, 12:13, 15:25; 1 Cor. 1:2, 6:1, 7:14; 2 Cor. 1:1; Eph. 3:8; Phil. 4:22; Col. 1:12, 22, 26; 1 Pet. 1:15-16. See also Taft, *Precommunion Rites*.

[281] Nicholas Cabasilas, *Commentary* 36:1-5 = *Explication de la divine liturgie*, ed. R. Bornert, J. Gouillard, and P. Périchon, SC 4bis (Paris: Cerf, 1967), 222-24; English translation in Taft, "Holy Things for the Saints," 90-91; see also Taft, *Precommunion Rites*.

communion of the one Lord Jesus and of the sanctity of the one God, who deigns to sanctify us all."[282]

The celebrant proclaims, Τὰ ἄγια τοῖς ἁγίοις ("Holy [things / gifts] for the holy"), which is simply two words in Slavonic: "Svjataja Svjatym!" The third iteration of "Holy" is in the congregation's response, "One is Holy…" (Greek: Εἷς ἄγιος…; Slavonic: Jedin Svjat…).[283] The prior English translation is "Holy things to the holy."[284]

The proposed change in the English here is not an improvement: "Holy gifts to holy people." [Unfortunately, this wording was promulgated in the revised Divine Liturgy.[285]] This seems a novel translation; at least I could not find it elsewhere.[286] "Things," while not euphonious, is reasonable and, importantly, unobtrusive. That is, in the phrase "holy things" clearly the important term remains "holy." Also, hitherto in English, in Slavonic, and in Greek the chant's final emphasis has been on the word "holy." The proposed revision would shift the emphasis to the word "people." But the emphasis belongs properly on the word "holy." Adding any other word to the end of this statement should be avoided. Any translation of this passage ought to "leave the nuances open for mystagogic catechesis and explanation," as well as meditation.[287] Regrettably, in the revision the musical emphasis is not on the essential word "holy" but on the added words, "gifts" and "people." That is, the music rises and is sustained for the words "gifts" and "people." Perhaps the revisers intended to make sure no one misunderstood what is referred to by the celebrant's final word "holy," but one wonders if anyone other than a casual visitor to Divine Liturgy had misunderstood it. One can be sure, however, that if the proposed revision is used, the faithful will become less likely to understand that "holy" is focal. The proposed revision sounds like ICEL, not the Slavonic Church. The Eastern Churches are familiar with living with mystery.

The remarks of Metropolitan Isaiah of Denver are germane:

---

[282] Taft, "Holy Things for the Saints," 91, citing Symeon of Thessalonika, *Exposition de Divino Templo* 91 (PG 155:741). See also Taft, *Precommunion Rites*.

[283] For the Greek, see *Divine Liturgy* (1983), 19. For the Slavonic, see *Divine Liturgy* (1978), 24.

[284] *Divine Liturgy* (1978), 24.

[285] [See the revised *Divine Liturgy* on p. 77.]

[286] Google, for instance, which locates 224 instances of "holy things for the holy," finds no occurrences of "Holy gifts to holy people," or "Holy gifts to holy," or "Holy gifts to the holy." Only 36 occurrences are found for "[the] holy gifts for the holy [people of God]."

[287] Keleher, *Response to the Proposed Recasting of the Byzantine-Ruthenian Liturgy* (as in note 6 above), pp. 235-36.

When the priest raises the Lamb and says, "Holy things for the holy," it is not necessary for him to add, "for the holy people of God." For whom did Christ come into the world? ...no amplification of Saint John Chrysostom's words is necessary. We know that Christ came into the world to restore His image in man.[288]

Further, he perceptively comments on such additions to the Divine Liturgy: "No one has the right to innovate the Divine Liturgy of Saint John Chrysostom. Could [the impulse to do so] be a touch of Protestantism, wherein everyone is an authority?"[289]

Hopefully the preposition of the proposed translation, "Holy things *to* the holy," will be modified, to become "Holy things *for* the holy." That translation (*for*) is frequently found (as witnessed in Metropolitan Isaiah's encyclical above), and it is also the version Fr. Taft uses.[290] It is also the version that, as of 2006, has been used for decades in the Metropolia. The phrase "the holy" (τοῖς ἁγίοις, *Svjatym*) is in the dative, so either "for" or "to" is grammatically feasible. If, when he chanted these words, the celebrant had already brought the Eucharist through the Royal Doors and was in the act of bringing them "to" the faithful and was also just about to physically communicate them "to" the faithful, then "to" would make the best sense. However, the celebrant is elevating the Eucharist in the sanctuary, while he is facing East and not facing the people, when he reverently proclaims that the Holy [things are present] for [the sake of] the holy. In this context, surely "for" makes better sense than "to." Indeed, it is difficult to imagine why the revisers of the Divine Liturgy introduced a different preposition here.

Moreover, the translation "Holy things for the holy" is also used in several other Eastern Churches, including Greek Orthodox, Russian Orthodox, Coptic, and Melkite, and it also is the translation found in several passages of the Ante-Nicene Fathers series. "Holy things for the Holy" was the theme of the Eucharistic Marian Congress of the Catholic Eparchy of Stamford, Connecticut, August 13-14, 2004. It is also the translation used in the document of the Synod of Bishops entitled "The Eucharist: Source and Summit of the Life and Mission of the Church" (May 28, 2004).[291]

Another possible translation of this liturgical call ought to be considered here: "Holy for the holy!" Such a translation would be radically Eastern, as close as possible to

---

[288] Metropolitan Isaiah, Greek Metropolis of Denver, Encyclical 12, October 29, 2003, item 20 (http://denver.goarch.org/teleturgical-encyclicals/te12.html).

[289] Ibid., item 11, concerning the personal practice of some priests of revising "Wisdom!" into "This is wisdom." See also items 13, on the introduction to the Epistle, and 18, on the consecration.

[290] Taft, *Precommunion Rites*, 234.

[291] Synod of Bishops, XI Ordinary General Assembly, § 43.

the Slavonic and Greek. The celebrant's words at the elevation are mysterious, and the English translation ought to honor that mystery. If anyone would object that "Holy for the holy" is hard to understand, and that hearing it would arrest the attention, then the reply may be that in truth it is hard to understand. The mystery is real.

10. *Irmos for the Annunciation*

The translation of this irmos is much changed, and three of the changes are fine. It is not clear, however, that the other changes are fitting. In the translation found in the *Byzantine Book of Prayer* (imprimatur: March 25, 1995) and in the *Divine Liturgy* (1978) the words are:

> Let no unclean hand touch the living Tabernacle of God; but let the lips of the faithful sing endlessly with joy to the Mother of God the greeting of the Angel: Hail, O Woman full of grace, the Lord is with you![292]

This is, of course, the same text in use in John Vernoski's settings of the irmos used regularly by our parish and presumably by many, if not most or all of the parishes of the Metropolia. The new translation introduced in the leaflets for the Annunciation in 2005 [and promulgated in 2007] is as follows:

> Let no uninitiated hand touch the living Ark of God; but let the faithful lips, singing without ceasing the words of the angel to the Theotokos, cry aloud in great joy: Rejoice, O Full of Grace, the Lord is with you![293]

It is wonderful and valuable to introduce into Ruthenian worship the Greek designation "Theotokos." The earlier English version's use of "Mother of God" where the Slavonic clearly had *Bohoróditsa* was Romanizing. "Theotokos" (or, of course, *Bohoróditsa*) is appropriate. Hopefully, however, there will not be a change to revise the non-liturgical hymn "O Godbearer Virgin" to "O Theotokos Virgin."[294] It is useful to have, within the entire body of hymnody, both "Theotokos" and "Godbearer," for exactly the same reason it is useful to have both "Pasch" and "Passover": The literal English term helps make clear the meaning of the transliterated one.

---

[292] *Divine Liturgy* (1978), 129.

[293] 2005 Great Friday Vespers, 40-41. [This is retained in the revised *Divine Liturgy* on pp. 330-31.]

[294] [That hymn, however, appears as "Rejoice, O Virgin Theotokos," in the revised *Divine Liturgy* on p. 453. The word *Bohoróditsa* does not appear in that hymn or anywhere else in the volume.]

As for Tabernacle/Ark, the Slavonic has the word *kivotos* which is the transliterated form of the Greek word for Ark (of the Covenant) used in the Septuagint.[295] Perhaps the lengthy word "Tabernacle" had been chosen over the monosyllable "Ark" for the prior translation for the sake of the cadence in English, to fill the musical role that the three-syllable word *kivotos* holds in Slavonic.

While "Hail" allowed clear affinities with our Roman Catholic neighbors, "Rejoice" is a customary English translation of the Slavonic *Radostiju*.[296] This is a welcome change.

Aside from these few changes, however, it is not clear that different wordings are necessary. A study of the full irmos in all its versions would be of interest. For instance, the Slavonic may well intend meaningful word play in "...*skvernych*. ... *že v'irnych*." At present, regarding the revised English version used on March 25, 2005, three points warrant comment.

a. "unclean." The language of "clean" and "unclean" goes back to the Torah. With regard to the sacrosanct Ark, no human hand, even one ritually clean, could be clean enough to touch it: For the perfection of the Ark of the Covenant, even a ritually clean human hand was, in a sense, unclean. So, the prior English version of the irmos makes sense when it refers to an "unclean hand." Similarly, one finds the following translation: "Let no profane hand touch the living Ark of God" used in N. Houston, Texas, at the Russian Orthodox Church of Saint Jonah of Manchuria.[297] In contrast, the modern term "uninitiated" seems to ignore the Jewish origins of the image of the Ark. How is one to understand "uninitiated hand" in relation to the Ark of the Covenant? There was no initiation which could make someone worthy to touch the Ark of the Covenant. Again, how is one to understand "uninitiated hand" in relation to Mary? What does "uninitiated hand" mean? Also the term "uninitiated" lacks Greek Catholic resonance.[298] It suggests instead a reduction of the Church into a merely social group.

---

[295] *Divine Liturgy* (1978), 129. The Hebrew word for the Ark (*aron*) of the Covenant (and various other chests, coffers, and coffins) is different from the Hebrew used for Noah's ark (*tebhah*) and the ark of bulrushes in which the infant Moses was saved. The Greek used κιβωτός for the Ark of the Covenant and for Noah's ark (e.g., Gen. 6:14, Exod. 25:10) but θῖβιν for the ark of bulrushes (Exod. 2:3).

[296] E.g., *Divine Liturgy* (1978), 78, 79, 81.

[297] http://www.saintjonah.org/lit/lit_entry.htm

[298] Despite the fact that one can find an Orthodox English translation of this Irmos using the word: "Let no *uninitiated* hand approach the living Ark of God to touch it," translated from the Russian by Anatoli Peredera, used at St. Gregory Palamas Monastery in Perrysville, Ohio: http://www.father alexander.org/booklets/english/blagov_e.htm

b. Theosis and the angel. Consider where precisely in the irmos the angel is mentioned. In this too the prior English version seems more authentically Byzantine and Ruthenian. Here reference not only to the Slavonic but to the traditions of Byzantine hymnody seems pertinent. Byzantine hymnody has definite characteristics, developed in order to facilitate the worship of the faithful and their theosis.[299] Often a hymn builds toward a final line which is a quotation, a statement in direct address, originally uttered by a saint or angel. Immediately before that final line the hymn identifies the original speaker. This pattern puts the faithful in the position of voicing again holy words spoken at an important moment in salvation history.[300] Thus with Eve we exclaim, "O Christ, it is you who give resurrection to all!" The earlier English translation of the irmos for the Annunciation follows this pattern, and indeed it does so better than the Slavonic. Thus we proclaim that we sing the "greeting of the Angel: Hail, O Woman full of grace, the Lord is with you!" and in proclaiming this, we recreate it in ritual. We, too, address Mary. The purpose for this recreation is like all the other recreations of the liturgy, to help the faithful seek to be sanctified, to animate our awareness that we live in the communion of saints.

c. Acknowledging the Woman. Regarding the angel's address to Mary, retaining the use of the noun "woman" makes better sense than dropping it.

Yes, it is quite true that the Greek (and Slavonic) word for "full" is an adjective and that no noun "woman" is present in the text. And there is at least one other English translation of a hymn with these words that omits the word "woman." However, the text of March 25, 2005, is the irmos of the Feast of the Annunciation, and as such there is a greater significance to how it is rendered into English, for it should be particularly close to the biblical text of Luke. This is not merely a historical nicety: The faithful are reenacting the Angel's words (Luke 1:28), and it is proper to provide those words as closely as is reasonable to the original. Besides, although Luke's Greek adjective (also the Slavonic adjective) indicates feminine gender, Modern English nouns do not indicate grammatical gender. To translate literally, one would have to say "Rejoice, [O Entity-designated-by-a-noun-of-feminine-gender] full of Grace." [Note that the revised *Divine Liturgy* does supply the word "woman" elsewhere, in headings on pp. 391, 399.] One reasonable translation is to supply the word "thou," as is done in this Irmos in at

---

[299] For examples in Greek, see Tkacz, "Singing Women's Words as Sacramental Mimesis" (as in note 86 above), 298-299 and notes 104-108. The Slavonic translations retain this pastoral pattern: It is seen, for instance, in the 1976 Great Friday Vespers, 39.

[300] Tkacz, "Singing Women's Words as Sacramental Mimesis," e.g., 299, 300-303.

least one Russian Orthodox Church: "Rejoice, thou who art full of grace."[301] A different solution is to supply the word "maiden": "Rejoice, Maiden full of grace."[302] Considering just this evidence, "woman" is certainly a reasonable translation to use in this Irmos.

Moreover, when the moment of salvation history is attentively noted, the reasons for retaining the word "woman" are seen to be much greater. The Angel's salutation comes moments before Mary voices her obedience to God's will and then, by the Holy Spirit, conceives the effable Word of God. Because the Angel addresses her, not by name, but in language calling attention to her womanhood, his words highlight the fact that it was in fact a woman who was the means of the Incarnation. Also, Jesus addressed His mother as "woman" (γύναι) at the wedding of Cana (John 2:4).

Within the full scope of salvation history, the importance of Mary's being a woman is even greater. The Angel's address to Mary without naming her, but identifying her as female, evokes, as the Fathers noted, the fact that the opening chapters of Genesis refer to Eve simply as "woman" until after the Fall.[303] Patristic and Byzantine discussions contrast Eve and Mary, often referring to each as "woman," in a manner which directs attention to what Pope John Paul II of blessed memory called the "iconic" nature of the female sex. The Fourth Sticheron for Great Compline before the Feast of the Nativity is a meditation based on these contrasts of the two women.[304] Mary as the New Eve continues to be recognized as important in the Church, most notably in *Munificentissimus Deus* by Pope Pius XII (November 1, 1950). Given this rich theological tradition of identifying Mary as "woman" at the Annunciation, then, it is best to include "Woman" in the words of the Angel in the irmos of the Annunciation.

Finally, at the start of the third millennium, when understanding and respecting women's capacities and contributions has a new urgency, it is important to honor the Theotokos as a woman. She is a model for every human being, male and female, in faith and obedience to the will of God. At the same time, as a woman, and blessed among women, she is a particular inspiration to women. The words of the Angel are a text that the Church ought not to make artificially generic by obscuring the femaleness of the Virgin.

---

[301] Saint Jonah Orthodox Church, N. Houston, Texas: http://www. saintjonah.org/lit/lit_entry.htm.

[302] This irmos, translated from the Russian by Anatoli Peredera, is used at St. Gregory Palamas Monastery in Perrysville, Ohio: http://www. fatheralexander. org/booklets/english/blagov_e.htm

[303] She is first named Eve in Genesis 3:20. The Byzantine contrasts of Eve and Mary are in, e.g., the Fourth Sticheron for Great Compline before the Feast of the Nativity.

[304] Tkacz, "Reproductive Science and the Incarnation" (as in note 43 above), 13-14.

Indeed, it is ironic that the materials of March 25, 2005, which apparently seek to show respect for women by using "humanity" instead of "man," also remove the word "Woman" from the irmos of the Annunciation.

Music

The musical changes warrant special attention, in addition to the comments above on specific musical settings. Over and over again musical changes have been introduced for, apparently, the sake of making the music different. This itself is counter to the authentic Byzantine approach to liturgical music. Where the music was good in the services of March 25, 2005, it was what has been used before. Where there were changes from the way the chant had been scored before, the new version was less recognizable as the tone intended, less effective in suiting the text, and less musical. In sum, it was less Slavic. New musical lines which were evidently meant to be elaborated for the feast were often only busy. Great reliance was evidently placed upon Bokshai and Malinich's 1906 volume of Prostopinije (Plain Chant), although it was originally done in Hungarian and then put back into Church Slavonic.[305] Although in part the music of March 25, 2005, was limited by the new, often inferior translations, the texts were only part of the problem, as will be seen.

The claim has frequently been made that there is no uniformity in how the parishes have been performing the Divine Liturgy, that musically there in fact is no norm. This is obviously overstated. Otherwise, how could it have happened that the Ukrainian Seminary in Rome sang the Divine Liturgy in Slavonic at St. Peter's Basilica on November 13, 1997, with the same music that I knew from worship at SS. Cyril and Methodius in Spokane, Washington? Also, in 1999, at the historically ecumenical celebration of the 75th anniversary of the Metropolitan Church of Pittsburgh, the Orthodox Metropolitan of Amissos participated. Afterwards, Metropolitan Nicholas observed:

> It was wonderful to note that the Prostopinije – Plain Chant – has not been replaced with any other liturgical musical expression. It was sung just as it is sung in our own Diocesan Church to this very day, and just as it is sung in the largest of cities and the tiniest of villages in our homeland![306]

---

[305] Bokshai and Malinich, *Tserkovnoe prostopienie* (as in note 153 above).

[306] Metropolitan Nicholas of Amissos, "Common Roots Run Deep," *The Church Messenger* (October 17, 1999). His editorial and many other documents exchanged between the Orthodox and our Byzantine Catholic Seminary are quoted in full in an article of the same name compiled and composed by Rev. John G. Petro, in *Eastern Churches Journal* 8.1 (2001): 11-38. The quotation is from p. 12.

Only for grave and serious cause ought we to sacrifice this unity among ethnic groups and of Eastern Catholic and Orthodox.

Comments are given here on the music of Psalm 140 and the hymns of Vespers. Additional remarks can be found below on the music of the Apostichera of Joseph of Arimathea, the Dismissal, on additional hymn-texts awkwardly matched to traditional hymn melodies, and on the use of non-liturgical melodies for proper parts of the Divine Liturgy.

1. Psalm 140

The musical changes here seem to be tinkering. Musically, the prior version seems better in each instance and as a whole.[307] Moreover, the results are unfortunate. Before, eloquently, the musical line for the words "Let my prayer be directed like incense to You" had risen to A for "prayer" and stayed up through the first syllable of the word "incense," then descending peacefully for the rest of the clause. Then, for "the lifting up of my hands as an evening sacrifice," the line had enacted a strong "lifting" by starting on F ("and the") and at once rising up a fourth to B for the entire phrase "lifting up of my hands." Again followed a graceful descent on the phrase "as an evening sacrifice." What a beautiful consonance of music with meaning. In the new setting, however, the word "incense" heavily descends in three half-notes (G, F, E) and then only the syllables "lift" and "up" attain a high pitch (B), with "of my hands" descending at once, as if the hands are heavy and must be lowered.[308] Musically, this is disappointing.

Often the beginnings and ends of the new musical settings are far less effective than the prior versions. Before, in the setting used for at least thirty years, the emphasis was on "not," sequent on the word "firm": "He has made the world firm, *not* to be moved." [309] Now, however, the word "to" is the melodic highpoint of "The world he made firm, not *to* be moved."[310]

Musically, it sounds as if a Western style of melisma has entered the Slavonic liturgy. The runs of notes for the second "depths" in the Prokimenon,[311] the extra flourishes in the Alleluia,[312] the conclusion of the Irmos,[313] and the see-saw run of notes

---

[307] Please refer to the 1976 version, 8, and the 2005 version, 10-11.

[308] 2005 Great Friday Vespers, 10-11.

[309] 1976 Great Friday Vespers, 32.

[310] 2005 Great Friday Vespers, 52.

[311] 2005 Great Friday Vespers, 26.

[312] 2005 Great Friday Vespers, 27.

in the final singing of "Hear me, O Lord" in Psalm 140,[314] sound like "mini-melismas" of a Gregorian sort. Such melismas are a feature of later Gregorian chant. Slavonic chant, like the Greek chant of Constantinople, had its own melismatic settings and book of melismatic choral chants called asmatikon.[315] But these seem rather different from the patterns introduced in the liturgy of March 25, 2005. Moreover, in every case – Gregorian, Greek, and Slavonic chant – it was professional singers, not parish cantors, who sang the melismatic chants, so that those elaborated chants had only a limited, specialized use. Slavonic chant tends to maintain a clear melodic line distinctive to the Tone being sung. It seems contrary to the tradition of Slavonic chant to obscure these melodic lines.

Slavonic melismas can be seen in some of the chants of "Alleluia" elaborated for important feast days. For instance, our parish has used in the past a more elaborate setting of the Tone 1 Alleluia for Mid-Pentecost Wednesday.[316] Importantly, that elaborate setting is still clearly the Tone 1 Alleluia. Also it is more musical that the Alleluia of March 25, 2005. Likewise, the Tone 6 Alleluia for the Liturgy for the Deceased is more elaborate, yet clearly Slavonic.[317] Repeatedly, the musical elaborations added to the Liturgy of March 25, 2005, are inadequate, and in two ways: 1) They are busy and awkward rather than effective, and 2) they obscure the melodic line of the tone they are intended to adorn.

Musically, another concern is the homogenized or regularized rhythm in the 2005 Great Friday / Annunciation service. This steady rhythm also appears to characterize music coming from the Metropolitan Cantor Institute. Dotted quarters and sixteenth notes and triplets are virtually gone.[318] Consistently the previous musical settings had more rhythmic variety. Such variety is found, for instance, in the printed materials from the Byzantine Seminary Press, in the musical leaflets from John Vernoski, and in the older

---

[313] 2005 Great Friday Vespers, 41. Compare *Divine Liturgy* (1978), 129.

[314] 2005 Great Friday Vespers, 10-11. Compare 1976 Great Friday Vespers, 8.

[315] On melismas in Greek and Slavonic chant, see Levy, "Slavic Kontakia and Their Byzantine Originals" (as in note 82 above).

[316] A former pastor of our parish several years ago made pew books that consisted of the printed Divine Liturgy of St. John Chrysostom from the Byzantine Seminary Press, followed by a table of contents to the following 394 handwritten scores of proper music prepared by Jerry Jumba and Msgr. Alexis Mahalik. In the upper right hand corner of each score was printed "BYZANTINE RITE / CARPATHO-RUSIN PLAINCHANT." At the bottom right corner of each page were the handwritten initials A.M., J.J. or A.M./J.J. The Alleluia, Tone 1, for Mid-Pentecost Wednesday is on 158.

[317] Ibid., 73.

[318] 2005 Great Friday Vespers: The exceptions are the Alleluia on p. 27, the Magnification on 40, the Nicodemus Hymns on 56, 58, 59, and the Dismissal on 60. The rhythmic sameness seems to be a sort of musical dumbing down.

pewbooks of our parish. These older pewbooks have, for instance, quarter notes, dotted half notes, and triplets in the setting of "Tjilo Christovo" ("Receive the Body of Christ"), and virtually every page has such rhythmic sophistication.[319]

Complex rhythms certainly seem to be native to our Slavonic chant tradition: They are in the earliest Slavonic musical manuscripts of the twelfth and thirteenth centuries.[320] Moreover, they are still in use, and not merely in the English and Slavonic our parish has been singing from its founding. Moreover, even if it could be shown that there was another old custom of chant that used a steady rhythm -- rarely using sixteenth notes or dotted notes or triplets, for instance -- I suggest that the rhythmically richer way already familiar to the faithful is a fitting, better way of matching English cadences to the Slavonic chant tones. Compared to the graceful setting of "Lord, have mercy" (e.g., a dotted quarter, a sixteenth note, and a quarter for "Lord"), the proposed settings are boring.[321] The prior version is much more effective.

Another consideration is important: It seems most likely that certain passages in the Divine Liturgy in English have preserved the detailed musical line of the Slavonic. For instance, *Hospodi pomiluj* provides not just the general musical line for "Lord, have mercy," but even the pattern of three notes for "Lord." Because "Hospodi" is three syllables, arrayed over three notes, the singing of the English translation "Lord" was also arrayed over the same three notes, with the rhythm suggested by the stress on the first syllable of "Hospodi." Because the Slavonic was chronologically first, it must have been the Slavonic that provided this pattern for use with the English translation. Today, chanting these words with identical music is an element that the Ruthenian Church worshiping in English has in common with, for instance, the Ukrainians in the seminary in Rome. It is important that we today preserve such shared elements of worship, unless grave cause requires a change. It is hard to imagine what such a cause might be.

2. Hymns of Vespers

"From the watch of dawn until the night, from the watch of dawn let Israel long for the Lord." In the prior setting of "let Israel long for the Lord" the music was apt, arching up to the line's highest pitch for word "long" and then descending gracefully

---

[319] "Tjilo Christovo": Jumba and Mahalik, "BYZANTINE RITE / CARPATHORUSIN PLAINCHANT," 54.

[320] Each of Levy's three musical examples from these manuscripts uses complex rhythms: Levy, "Slavic Kontakia and Their Byzantine Originals."

[321] 2005 Great Friday Vespers, 9.

into musical resolution. [322] In the new setting, the words are dumbed down to "count on" and the word emphasized by the high pitch is "the."[323]

3. *The Apostichera of Joseph of Arimathea*

These also hold musical changes and many verbal ones.[324] The vivid "torn asunder" is replaced by "torn in two." "Behold" and "beseech" are avoided like dirty words. Surprisingly, the simple words "death" and "body" are less frequent in the new translation. Christians adore the incarnate Lord, and when is it more fitting to mention His death and His lifeless body than on Great and Holy Friday? The old version had used a sustained high note for "body" where the new version lacks the word entirely.[325] "Grace" and "gracious" are words that belong to the faithful through the ages, and it is wrong to expunge them from our authentic worship. Is "compassionate" really a better translation than "gracious"? Musically, the conclusion of the full set of Apostichera is so much better in the prior version.[326]

The procession with the shroud is accompanied by the Troparion "The noble Joseph...." This was superior in the prior version. It had a more regular rhythm, suitable for a procession. It also musically emphasizes the body of Christ (and in this it follows the Slavonic better than the 2005 version). For logical order, the 1976 version is better: One anoints a body before covering it in cloth. In the 2005 version of this song, as in so much else, the changes of text and music seem unneeded and pointlessly distracting.

The final troparion's doxology in the 2005 version (p. 59) conforms to the melodic ending used throughout the processional kontakion. In itself that is lovely, but it does mean that every line in the troparion and kontakion ends identically. I suspect the simpler setting[327] was more effective in giving a clear end to the procession, by being musically different.

---

[322] 1976 Great Friday Vespers, 11.

[323] 2005 Great Friday Vespers, 14-15.

[324] 2005 Great Friday Vespers, 51-56. "Torn in two": p. 55. "Compassionate": p. 56. The prior liturgical book had "gracious Lord," p. 35.

[325] Old Great and Holy Friday Vespers, 34: A dotted half on C and a quarter note on B for the word "body." Compare 2005 Great Friday Vespers, 54.

[326] 1976 Great and Holy Friday Vespers, 35-36.

[327] 1976 version, p. 38.

It seems silly to avoid the word "reveal" and substitute "show."[328]

4. *Dismissal and the reality of blessing*

Up until now, the congregation's response during the Dismissal – the doxology and, immediately, the people's call for the final blessing -- has been a coherent musical line that still respected the fact that two different actions are occurring. That is, the Doxology has been sung on a sustained A, a sustained G, back to sustained A, and then a new pitch, B, is used for the request to the celebrant, with this request resolving to A. Yet even this simple line has been altered in the 2005 version. The change disregards the fact that liturgically the doxology is different from the address to the celebrant. In the 2005 version (p. 61) the whole passage alternates between A and G. [329]

That change in the dismissal on March 25, 2005, is like the numerous changes introduced into the Roman Rite in America in recent decades: These changes minimize the reality of blessing. This is not a minor point. In every liturgy of every rite, Catholic or Orthodox, the celebrant and the faithful exchange blessings. These blessings are real bestowals of grace. Our sung Divine Liturgy shows the reality of these blessings better than the spoken, pruned verbal versions in the Roman Rite today. It is significant that in many Roman parishes, even the priest or bishop has forgotten that the exchange of blessing is real and important, so that after the initial exchange of blessings the celebrant often interjects "Good morning!" and the people are expected to reply "Good morning!" On March 25, 2005, the musical setting of the dismissal showed just such a failure to recognize the reality of blessing and the importance of the role of the faithful in the liturgy.

5. *Additional hymn texts*

A word must be said also about the additional non-liturgical hymn-texts sometimes being produced recently in the Metropolitan Cantor Institute. These are not texts to be chanted as part of the liturgy proper, but optional hymns used during communion, for instance. Only someone who is a theologian, poet, and perhaps a mystic ought to attempt such lyrics. Merely putting new words to traditional melodies is not enough.

---

[328] Cf. 1976 version, p. 38, to 2005, p. 59.

[329] A (*Glory be to the Father and the Son and to the Holy Spir-*), G (*-it, now and ever and forever A-*), A (*-men. Lord, have mercy. Lord, have mercy. Lord, have mercy*). B (*Give the bless-*), A (*-ing*). [The only change in this in the revised *Divine Liturgy* is that in the final iteration of the word "mercy" the second syllable is sung on the B with the words "Give the bless-": see p. 89.]

A case in point is the recently written "Hymn of SS. Cyril and Methodius," sung to the traditional melody of "Kol Slaven Naš." That melody is well-known, even venerable. The new text, however, is mediocre and does not fit the music particularly well.[330] Especially poor is the last stanza, referring to the saints' "dream" and rhyming that with "plot and scheme." When I first heard these lyrics in May, 2005, when Professor Sebastian Brock delivered the Seminary's annual SS. Cyril and Methodius Lecture, the refrain had been set quite awkwardly to the music. After I pointed this out in a letter and observed what the natural assignments of words to notes would be, the text was reassigned to the notes more tunably, exactly as I had suggested. To be specific: The Slavonic refrain begins "Vezd' i Hospod', vezd'i on slaven." Originally the refrain of the new song had begun "For CYR-il AND MeTHO-o-di-US, Lord." Because the rhythm of the words was at odds with the musical rhythm, a wooden regularity resulted. Even if one were determined to set those words to that music, the obvious musical choice for the ending would be: "For CYR-il AND Me-THO-di-us, LO-rd." That is essentially how the revised setting runs: "For CYR-il AND Me-THO-di-us, LORD, your" with the sentence completed in the final line of the refrain. [331]

But the hymn-text remains pedestrian. Moreover, it was thoughtless and even offensive to use the holy name "Lord" at the end of a line to provide a rhyme for "afford." Byzantine hymnody never plugs in divine names as filler. Similarly, Dante in his entire Divine Comedy used *Cristo* as a rhyme word rarely, and only in *Paradiso*, and the only word he deemed worthy to rhyme with it was itself, *Cristo*.[332] Byzantine hymns ought to be equally reverent in the use of names for God. Several new song-texts have come forth from the Metropolitan Cantor Institute, and they are weak theologically and poetically.

It is useful at this point to treat non-liturgical song in the Slavonic Church, in order to set in context some final remarks on recent musical innovations proposed for the Ruthenian Church.

Excursus on non-liturgical song

Byzantine liturgical music consists entirely of chant. From antiquity certain psalms have been chanted for communion hymns. This practice of course remains valid,

---

[330] This is also true of another new hymn text from the Metropolitan Cantor Institute, set to the music "To Jordan's Water." Reputedly the other new hymn texts from that source share the same problems.

[331] This revised setting is on p. 27 of a booklet, "Moleben to Our Holy Fathers Cyril and Methodius," prepared at SS. Cyril and Methodius Byzantine Catholic Seminary, [2006?].

[332] *Paradiso* 12.71, 73, 75; 14.104, 106, 108; 19.104, 106, 108; 32.83, 85, 87.

even though now some non-liturgical songs can also be sung during reception of the Eucharist. Like the Psalms and the Divine Liturgy in Greek, the original Slavonic liturgical texts are without meter and rhyme. Although meter and rhyme are characteristic of poetic compositions of medieval and modern Europe, they are rarely found in Eastern liturgical texts. An authentic development of the Greek liturgy was that a few specific liturgical chants gained additional roles as optional communion hymns during the liturgy. There appears to be a Slavonic counterpart to this, as will be seen. But non-liturgical song-tunes are not to be used as musical settings for liturgical texts.

a. **Liturgical songs that gained additional uses.** Some liturgical chants over time acquired additional roles, often as a communion hymn, roles beyond their original purpose. Such happened to the Vespers Hymn of Great Thursday, the Magnificat, and the Byzantine precursor to the "Hail, Mary."

i. **Great Thursday Vespers Hymn: Τοῦ Δείπνου σου.** In the sixth century, the Vespers Hymn from Great and Holy Thursday, "Τοῦ Δείπνου σου" (*Tou deipnou sou*; in Latin: *Cenae tuae*) began to be used as a communion hymn throughout the year in the monasteries.[333] Certainly this hymn in Slavonic, "*Večeri tvojeja tajnyja dnes'*" ("Let me this day"), is part of the Ruthenian liturgy for Great and Holy Thursday: In the 1976 liturgical books of the Pittsburgh Metropolia it is sung three times on that Thursday, namely, in lieu of the Cherubikon, as the Communion hymn, and instead of "May our lips be filled."[334] For several years it was also sung at each celebration of the Divine Liturgy as a communion hymn.

Note that this text has neither rhyme nor meter, and these features help indicate its antiquity.

ii. **Magnificat and Θεοτόκος παρθένος.** It appears likely that a similar history occurred with the words of Elizabeth and the Theotokos. Certainly Elizabeth's words to the Theotokos at the Visitation became the prayer of the faithful in both East and West. Praying her acclamation evidently began in the East: a troparion ("Χαῖρε κεχαριτωμένη Θεοτόκε") based on the words of Gabriel and Elizabeth seems to

---

[333] Robert F. Taft, S.J., "The Pontifical Liturgy of the Great Church according to a Twelfth-century Diataxis in Codex British Museum Add. 34060," *Orientalia Christiana Periodica* 45 (Rome, 1979), 279-307, at 300-306 and 46 (Rome, 1980), 89-124, at 118; reprinted in Robert F. Taft, S.J., *Liturgy in Byzantium and Beyond* (Aldershot, Eng., 1995). See also Thomas Schattauer, "The Koinonicon of the Byzantine Liturgy: An Historical Study," *Orientalia Christiana Periodica* 49.1 (1983), 91-129, at 109-10, 112; and Joseph Szövérffy, *A Guide to Byzantine Hymnography: A Classified Bibliography of Texts and Studies*, 2 vols. (Brookline, Mass., 1978); 1:94. On the migration of "Τοῦ Δείπνου σου" into the Milanese Liturgy, see Anton Baumstark, *Comparative Liturgy*, rev. B. Botte, O.S.B., trans. F. L. Cross (Westminster, Md., 1958).

[334] *Divine Liturgy of St. Basil with Vespers for Great Thursday* [cover title: *Divine Liturgy with Vespers for Holy and Great Thursday*] (Pittsburgh: Byzantine Seminary Press, 1976), pp. 25, 30, 32.

go back to the fourth or fifth century.[335] The phrase Θεοτόκος παρθένος (*Theotokos parthenos*, in Slavonic: *Bohorodice Djivo*) was added, sometimes with the name Mary, as is known from sixth-and seventh-century ostraka.[336] The Byzantine troparion appears in the Feast of the Nativity of Our Lady as the antiphon for the Magnificat.[337] Thus the biblical texts of the angelic greeting, of Mary's Magnificat, and of Elizabeth's greeting became liturgical chant texts. The Magnificat and most of the chant based on the words of Elizabeth consist of quotation from the Gospels. In time both of these chants became used as Marian hymns. That is, they appeared outside their original liturgical settings.[338]

It is worth calling attention to the fact that these Marian chant texts, too, are without meter and rhyme.

b. Chant-inspired vernacular compositions. In Slavonic worship, it may well have been that from time to time a certain chant tone associated with a particular liturgical season would fire the imagination of a poet, who composed a vernacular poem, using characteristic features of Slavonic poetry, and set it to what was essentially that chant tone. Thus rhyme and poetic meter became part of paraliturgical Slavonic hymns. Because the song-text followed a characteristically Slavonic poetic structure, the melody for the resulting religious song is more structured than is the original chant tone. The new religious song was never properly part of the Divine Liturgy, in the way that a troparion or the Our Father is, but it came into use as a hymn, and today is among the repertoire of communion hymns.

i. Slavonic Christmas Songs: *Divnaja Novina* **and** *Nova Radost' Stala.* It appears likely that chant tones specific to the Nativity of the Lord inspired the creation of one or more Christmas songs. Specifically, the chant used at the Nativity for the Cherubikon seems to be the source for the melody of the Slavonic Christmas song *Divnaja*

---

[335] Jean Laurenceau, O.P., "Les débuts de la récitation privée de l'antienne 'Ave Maria' en occident avant la fin du XI siècle," *De Cultu Mariano saeculis VI-XI: Acta Congressus Mariologici-Marianni Internationalis in Croatia anno 1971 celebrati*, ed. Gérard Philips (Rome, 1972), vol. 2: *Considerationes generales*, 231-46, at 235. Soon afterwards in the West, from the sixth century onwards, the angel's greeting to Mary was the antiphon for the fourth Sunday of Advent; in 1261 Pope Urban IV coupled the angelic greeting with Elizabeth's greeting: David Siegenthaler, "Popular Devotion and the English Reformation: The Case of *Ave Maria*," *Anglican and Episcopal History* 6.1 (1992), 1-11, at 2.

[336] Laurenceau, "'Ave Maria' en occident," 235.

[337] Baumstark, *Comparative Liturgy*, 99.

[338] For these hymns in Slavonic see *Marian Hymnal*, pp. 28-35 and 18-19. Only the Magnificat, among all the songs in the hymnal, has the instruction, "in speaking style without rushing" (*Jak hovorjači ale naturalno*), p. 28, upper right corner. This direction marks the origin of the song as liturgical chant.

Novina ("Wondrous News").[339] Unlike the examples just seen – the Great Thursday Vespers Hymn, the Magnificat, and the Troparion based on Gabriel's words to Mary – this text, *Divnaja Novina*, is a new vernacular composition with meter and rhyme: The first, second, and fourth lines rhyme; those lines are also alike metrically, for each consists of three iambs, while the fourth line is longer. There is also internal rhyme in verse 7: *Vo pustyňi, vo jaskiňi*. The word for "Bethlehem" prevented such rhyme in the first stanza. The rhyming syllables are emboldened here:

> Divnaja no**vina**.
> Nyňi D'iva **Syna**.
> Porodila v Viflejemi
> Marija je**dina**.
>
> Ne v carskoj pa**laťi**.
> No meždu byd**ľati**,
> Vo pus**tyňi**, vo jas**kiňi**,
> Treba to vs'imn **znati**.

The music for this hymn is well-suited to its pattern of rhyme, for the music has identical first and second lines, a quite different third line, and a fourth line which is a variation of the first and second.

Other Christmas songs may well have been inspired by chant tones. *Nova Radost' Stala* ("Joyful News") uses what appears to be a melodic development of chant, and it has been used to set communion hymns (Psalm 148 and Psalm 32) at the feasts of the Holy Forefathers and of the Nativity. [340] This Christmas song, too, is a new Slavonic composition with meter and rhyme: In fact, its poetic structure is identical to that of "Wondrous News":

> Nova radosť **stala**,
> Jaka ne by**vala**,
> Nad vertepom, zv'izda jasna
> Svitom zasi**jala**.

---

[339] *Christ Is Born: Glorify Him!* Adapted from traditional Byzantine Slavonic chants for congregational use, published with ecclesiastical approbation, compiled and published by Rev. William Levkulic (8 1969), pp. 19, 20 for the liturgical chants, p. 23 for the Christmas song.

[340] The song: *Christ Is Born*, 26. Please note that the Slavonic verses printed under the score are in a different order than are the English verses printed within the score: *Anhely* begins the third verse, following the English order. The liturgical settings of the psalms cited are seen in liturgical materials prepared for the parishes by John Vernoski and dated 11/89.

Anhely spivajut'.
"Slava" vosklicajut'.
Na nebesi i na zemli
Radost' vozviščajut'.

Kol' Christos rodilsja.
Z D'ivy voplotilsja.
Jak čelovik pelenami
Uboho povilsja.

The music for *Nova Radost' Stala* follows this pattern: After the first line of music, the pitch goes up one third and the musical first line is repeated at the higher pitch. The third line is quite different. Most of the fourth line is also quite different, although the final three notes reprise the final three notes of the first line and on the same pitches.

For these songs, the chant tones were adapted and made regular to fit metrically structured poetry. Their poetic structure and the affinities of their melodic lines to familiar chants suggest that a number of the Slavonic Christmas songs, such as *Divnaja Novina* and *Nova Radost' Stala*, may well have developed in the fourteenth-through-seventeenth centuries. Certainly the pattern of rhyme structure and the use of inflected verb endings to provide rhymes of two or three syllables are seen, for instance, in several Polish poems on biblical subjects written in the fifteenth and sixteenth centuries by authors including Jan Kochanowski and Erazm Otwinowski.[341]

ii. Other liturgy-inspired songs: *Vs'i T'a chory*. The song *Vs'i T'a chory* was obviously inspired by the text of the liturgical Cherubic Hymn and by the celebrant's introduction to it (and, of course, by Isaiah's underlying vision). The celebrant refers to the "countless angels and archangels," identifying the cherubim and seraphim, who stand before the Lord, singing "Holy, Holy, Holy." Similarly the song (in English) refers to "Countless angels on high" praising God in those same words, and (in Slavonic) actually identifies the heavenly host as angels, cherubim and seraphim, the words used in the liturgy to identify them. The angelic praise is the refrain: The threefold Holy, Holy, Holy, is augmented by the three names of the Trinity (Lord God, Christ God, Holy Spirit), and capped by the word "Sabaoth" reported by Isaiah as part of the angels' praise. Evidently the song was composed as a communion hymn. That is, it was not itself a proper part of the liturgy, and its music is not properly speaking liturgical chant; it is rather a paraliturgical hymn, with a melody close to chant. Of the songs considered here, this is the first one presented that has what can be called a chorus or refrain, although it is perhaps very close to being an antiphon.

---

[341] See, for instance, Jan Kochanowski, *Zusanna* (Kraków, 1564), reprint in *Dziela polski* (Warszawa, 1955), pp. 99-106; and Erazm Otwinowski, *Sprawy abo Historyje znacznych niewiast* (Kraków, 1589).

Vs'i T'a **chory**,

Nebes **dvory**,

Trojce, slavjat.

Svyat, svjat, svjat Hospod Boh,

Svyat, svjat, svjat Christos Boh,

Svyat, svjat, svjat Duch Svjatyj

Savaot.

Cheru**vimy**,

Sera**fimy**

Vosklicajut:

Svyat, svjat, svjat Hospod Boh,

Svyat, svjat, svjat Christos Boh,

Svyat, svjat, svjat Duch Svjatyj

Savaot.[342]

This is a Slavic meditation on the angelic praises. Isaiah recounted that the seraphim continuously praise God, crying out "Holy, holy, holy!" (Isaiah 6:17), and John in his Apocalypse records the same threefold praise of God by the hosts of heaven (Apoc. 4:8). The Catholic and Orthodox Eucharistic liturgies echo this praise, with the celebrant recalling that the ranks of angels sing this praise and we join with them. The chorus of the Slavic communion hymn seen here repeats the threefold "holy, holy, holy" for each person of the Trinity. Each verse has a Trinitarian three lines, also. This hymn is also notable in using the transliterated Hebrew words for cherubim, seraphim, and Sabaoth, and the Slavic word for Trinity (*Trojce*).

Musically, the first two lines of the three-line stanza are identical. The third is quite different. In the four-line refrain, each line is different. Its second and third lines successively start on higher pitches; the fourth line returns to the refrain's opening pitch.

---

[342] *Divine Liturgy* (1978), p. 150.

c. **Vernacular compositions.** Completely Slavic religious songs also arose, in which the text and music appear to be composed, rather than adapted from liturgical texts and chant. Their initial composition may well have been oral. Some of the Christmas songs are blithe and with spirited musical lines not usual in the Divine Liturgy outside of Pascha itself (although a brief exception is found during Strasti on Great and Holy Friday).[343] These original Slavic Christmas songs have refrains with a fixed poetic text, that is, with the same words sung after each stanza, and this is in contrast to *Divnaja Novina* ("Wondrous News") and *Nova Radost' Stala* ("Joyful News"). The Christmas song *Nebo i Zeml'a* ("Heaven and Earth") is a good example of such a vernacular composition.[344] Distinctive musically, it uses the same melodic line with identical meter twice through for the stanza.[345] The refrain is different, even in a different tempo (two-four, not the three-four tempo of the verse). Yet the refrain uses in its last 6 measures the same progression of notes from measures 1-4. It comes naturally to sing the refrain more briskly than the verse in this song, and the same is true of *Boh Predvičnyj* ("Eternal God").[346] Broadly, the same musical pattern underlies *Christos Rodilsja; Boh Voplotilsja* ("Rejoice All Nations"): The verse uses the same melodic line twice, the refrain contains quicker notes, and the conclusion of the refrain echoes the music of the last three measures of the verse.[347] This Christmas song also, however, has unique musical features,

---

[343] Then after the ninth Gospel the liturgical hymn ("Let everything that hath breath, praise the Lord!) echoes the praises of the psalms and could certainly be sung joyously and with a quicker tempo than the rest of the liturgy that day. That hymn of praise may well be a liturgical refrigerium, in anticipation of Easter, for in that hymn joyous psalm quotations alternate with somber passages voiced by Christ and Mary at the Crucifixion. See *Strasti --Matins for Holy and Great Friday* (Pittsburgh: Byzantine Seminary Press, 1976), pp. 31-33. Generally speaking, blitheness or merriness more often characterizes certain non-liturgical Christmas songs, than liturgical music.

[344] *Christ Is Born!* p. 22.

[345] Measures 1-4 are echoed in measures 5-8, except that the last note changes, going down, to mark the end of the verse.

[346] *Christ Is Born!* p. 24.

[347] *Christ Is Born!* p. 28. Although the written direction with the song indicates it is to be sung "Slowly," this may be a modern interpretation.

for the refrain itself is two-part, with two different melodic lines within it.[348] The music for the spirited Christmas songs sounds like medieval dance music. This suggests that they were composed in the fourteenth or fifteenth century.

The rhyme patterns of several of these Christmas songs are also characteristic of vernacular poetry from Eastern Europe. The song *Boh Sja Raždajet* ("God's Son is Born"), for instance, has end rhyme on the first two lines, and then both end rhyme and internal rhyme for the next three lines, and a playful concluding line (*"Tutže, tutže, tutže, tutže, tut!"*).[349] (The English does not reproduce the demanding vernacular rhyme pattern.) The original rhyme pattern fits the music perfectly; clearly they were composed together.

To summarize, several of the Slavic Christmas carols appear to be quite old, certainly pre-modern. Many of the songs have musical complexity while being memorable and singable.

Overall, and including the songs mentioned above, an extensive repertoire of non-liturgical songs developed in the Ruthenian Church over the centuries. Some honor Christ and some are for specific occasions. "To Jordan's Water" is a set of additional verses for *Nebo i Zeml'a*, extending the use of that Christmas hymn for Theophany; the date of the additional verses appears to be unknown. Other hymns are addressed to the Virgin. Some of these latter are among the most modern of the songs used in the Ruthenian Church.

d. Modern Marian songs. Unlike the Magnificat, which is ancient, and the *Bohorodice Djivo*, which may well be several centuries old, most of the Marian songs, such as *Prizri, O Marije* ("Mary Look upon Us") are evidently compositions from the eighteenth century or later and were originally composed as pilgrimage music, to be sung while walking to the Marian Shrine of Marija Povč (Mary of Povch), which became

---

[348] In the refrain, measure 2 echoes measure 1 and measures 7-8 echo measures 5-6; measures 3-4 and 9-10 are musically identical, and they echo the musical ending of the verse.

[349] *Christ Is Born!* p. 27.

important after 1696.[350] That is, these songs are the fruit of the last three hundred years.[351] They are much younger than the liturgical chant, and they also appear to be more recent than several hymns mentioned above. Clearly at least the song *Palonniki Uniontowns'ki* ("Come to Uniontown") was composed in or after 1934, when The Shrine of the Mother of Perpetual Help was blessed and dedicated on the hills of Mount Saint Macrina, Uniontown, Pennsylvania.[352] These compositions are characterized, in their modern editions at least, by a regular rhythm which befits music for use while walking. Often the stanza consists of two verses, sung to exactly the same melodic line, and the refrain may show the same pattern.[353] In some cases, every measure of the song has the same rhythm: For instance, every measure of *Božaja Mati, Čista Djivice* ("Purest of Virgins") consists of a quarter note, two eighth notes, then two quarter notes.[354] These songs have far greater regularity than liturgical chant, because the texts for the songs are modern poetic compositions, strictly patterned by meter. In contrast, Slavonic liturgical texts are usually prose and therefore chanting them produces rhythms closer to speech. The difference between the true chant of the Magnificat and, in contrast, most of the other songs in the Marian Hymnal is reflected in the fact that only the Magnificat is marked to be sung "in speaking style without rushing" (*Jak hovorjači ale naturalno*).[355]

Seventeen of the twenty-eight hymns in the popular *Marian Hymnal* issued by the Byzantine Seminary Press in 1984 have what appears to be a modern musical structure,

[350] *Marian Hymnal* (Pittsburgh: Byzantine Seminary Press, 1984), p. [i]. The persons who provided the words and music are identified on p. [ii]. Each song is identified as Carpathian Russian chant (*Kar. Rus'koje Pinije*), e.g., p. 34, upper right corner.

[351] Some of the songs in the *Marian Hymnal* are older. Certainly the Magnificat and *Bohorodice Djivo* are. The hymn for the Protection of Mary (October 1), *Djivo Mati, Zastupaj Nas* ("Virgin Mother, Intercessor"), on pp. 46-47, in its metrical intricacy sounds relatively older, and it has less rhyme.

[352] *Marian Hymnal*, pp. 8-9. For date, see p. [i].

[353] For instance, see the songs in *Marian Hymnal*, 2-5, 8-17, 20-23, 26-27, 38-39, 52-59.

[354] *Marian Hymnal*, 36-37. See also the pattern of "quarter note, half note" throughout the entire song, *"Pod tvoj pokrov"* ("We hasten to your patronage"), pp. 52-53.

[355] *Marian Hymnal*, p. 28, upper right corner.

intended to facilitate prolonged walking during pilgrimage. This sets them apart from the older hymns in the booklet, hymns without meter or rhyme and with non-formulaic music.[356] The seventeen hymns which appear modern consist of four musical lines each, and frequently some of the lines are identical within a given song. In "Come to Uniontown," for instance, the first and fourth line of music are identical and the third line differs from them only in the last two notes.[357] Frequently, as in *Radujsja Carice, prekrasna Djivce* ("[Rejoice,] Beautiful Holy Queen"), the first, second, and fourth lines of music are absolutely identical.[358] In fifteen more hymns the second musical line is an exact repeat of the first.[359] There are no musical subtleties, as in *Nova Radost Stala*. No metrical changes, as in *Vs'i T'a Chory'* or *Christos Rodilsja*. No tempo changes as in *Nebo i Zeml'a*.

In contrast to what certainly appear to be older Slavonic music, often based on chant, the evidence of text and music for these seventeen hymns suggests that they are fairly modern. Beloved as some of these modern Marian hymns may be, they are not liturgical chant. They nourish the religious tradition of the Slavs, without being technically part of the Divine Liturgy. Therefore it is not appropriate to use non-liturgical songs and their melodies as if they were liturgical.

7. Non-liturgical melodies are not to be used for liturgical texts

Recently, however, it appears that by innovation some parts of the Divine Liturgy are being set musically to non-liturgical melodies. This is seen in the expanded version of the proposed new liturgical materials for the Metropolia, which includes a variety of

---

[356] Older hymns include the Magnificat with Slavonic Pripiv, called "Praise of the Most Holy Godbearer" (pp. 28-33). "Pod Tvoju Milost'" (pp. 22-23) and "Preslavnaja Prisnodjívo Maríje" (pp. 22-23) are both Slavonic translations of prayers, without meter and rhyme, and their music is specific to them. "O Maríje Mati Vsích" (pp. 14-15) has some musical sophistication. "Bohorodice Djívo" has no rhyme and no repetition of musical lines (although one may compare measures 5 and 8).

[357] *Marian Hymnal*, pp. 8-9.

[358] *Marian Hymnal*, pp. 4-5.

[359] *Marian Hymnal*, pp. 1-2, 10-11, 12-13, 16-17, 26-27, 34-35, 38-39, 42-43, 46-47, 48-49, 50-51, 52-53, 54-55, 56-57, 58-59.

alternate musical settings of various parts of the Divine Liturgy sung by the faithful. In October of 2006 I saw briefly a revised liturgy booklet in use at SS. Cyril and Methodius Byzantine Catholic Seminary in Pittsburgh.[360] With considerable surprise, I saw that non-liturgical melodies were used in the booklet for proper parts of the Divine Liturgy.

During the Liturgy I attended in 2006, two such melodies were used. Even the Our Father was sung to the melody of a non-liturgical hymn, one frequently sung during the Great Fast. Although that hymn is familiar, it is not liturgical chant. Therefore it is not appropriate as a setting for the liturgical singing of the Our Father. Moreover, during that October liturgy in Pittsburgh the liturgical text "We praise you, we bless you" was set to a popular, modern Marian hymn tune, "Mary, Look upon Us" (*Prizji O Maríje*).[361]

[This remains true in the revised *Divine Liturgy*.[362] That volume's Foreword, signed by the four hierarchs of the Metropolia, states that the volume uses "plainchant settings." Evidently that is not always the case.]

[In addition to "We praise you, we bless you," the Cherubikon itself – "Let us who mystic'ly represent the cherubim" and "That we may receive the King of all" – has now been promulgated as set to that popular, apparently modern Marian hymn.[363] That Marian hymn, however, is not an integral part of the liturgy. Rather it is an optional hymn, an occasional hymn. It is quite inappropriate for its melody to be used within the Divine Liturgy as if it were liturgical chant. Analogously, it would be like singing the "Our Father" to the melody of "Silent Night." That carol, composed in 1816 by the Austrian priest Joseph Mohr, may be beloved, but it is not liturgical chant. It is important to distinguish between beloved cultural traditions and customs, on the one hand, and

---

[360] The booklets were for use on the premises, not for removal for study, so my remarks about them are necessarily brief.

[361] For the hymn, see *Marian Hymnal*, 12-13.

[362] In the revised *Divine Liturgy* , this setting is found on p. 60 as option F.

[363] See the revised *Divine Liturgy* , pp. 47, 48.

authentic liturgical practice, on the other. Although "Mary, Look upon Us" is a manifestation of Ruthenian culture, it is not liturgical chant.]

[Another repeated and dubious use in the revised *Divine Liturgy* of the music of the same popular hymn, "Mary, Look upon Us," is in new settings of three Psalms. Psalm 148:1, a traditional communion hymn for use every Sunday – "Praise you the Lord, the Lord of Heaven" – is now set to the melody of "Mary, Look upon Us."[364] Likewise another traditional communion hymn, Psalm 111:6, appears with that inappropriate musical setting in the service for "Two or More Venerable Women."[365] Again, Psalm 32:1, "Rejoice in the Lord," is set to the melody of "Mary, Look upon Us" as the communion hymn for "One Woman-Martyr." [366] While communion hymns are optional and paraliturgical, nonetheless it is strange to invent a new non-traditional musical setting for the ancient hymn texts from the Psalter, especially given that the revised *Divine Liturgy* purports to be restoring traditions, not playing with them.]

True, there is an outmoded tradition in Western Europe, in vogue in the sixteenth century, of capitalizing on the popularity of certain songs by using their musical themes as the basis for elaborate musical settings of the Mass.[367] The most popular song of the sixteenth century, for instance, Orlando di Lasso's "*Susanne un jour*,"[368] was used as a

---

[364] See the revised *Divine Liturgy* , on p. 81.

[365] See the revised *Divine Liturgy* , on pp. 399-401. The generic masculine of that verse has been altered to "The just woman...."

[366] See the revised *Divine Liturgy* , on pp. 391, 393.

[367] Entirely different is the use of secular melodies for non-liturgical hymns, which may have begun in the time of St. Ambrose. There are famous examples of drinking songs being used as the melodies for hymns, for instance, "I Feel the Winds of God Today." But these melodies were borrowed for non-liturgical hymns, they were not used to set proper parts of Orthodox or Catholic liturgies.

[368] "Susanne un jour," poem (1548) by Guillaume Guéroult, Lasso's setting first published 1560: *Mellange d'Orlande de Lassus* (Paris, 1570; reprint London: Pro Musica, 1983). Many of its numerous settings are discussed by Kenneth Jay Levy, "'*Susanne un Jour*': The History of a Sixteenth Century Chanson," *Annales musicologiques* 1 (1953) 375-401.

source for melodies for a mass.[369] The popular music exploited in this way was often secular in theme: "whole masses [were] arranged from Mozart's operas – one in particular being known as a "Missa di Figaro." Similarly, "a love duet of Mendelssohn's (Op. 63, No. 1) [was matched] to words about 'Spirits washed in the blood of Christ,'" an oddity which prompted a British musicologist to remark, "the Church shows strange taste in sanctioning such foolish mixtures."[370] But that practice of using non-liturgical music for liturgical texts was Western. It appears that there is no evidence that the practice ever spread to the Eastern churches. To the contrary, given the Eastern churches' abiding recognition of the fitness of chant for worship, it seems likely that the modish masses would have been scorned as irreligious, regardless of how impressive or elegant their musical compositions may have been.

[In sum, the use of non-liturgical music in place of chant within the revised Divine Liturgy is not in accordance with Eastern liturgical practice. To the contrary, it is a voluntary Americanization imposed by the hierarchy upon the faithful.]

[How disconcerting that a widesweeping revision of the Ruthenian Rite which is presented as restoring authentic practices includes such schmalzy innovations as setting the congregation's liturgical affirmation, "We praise you, we bless you," the Cherubikon itself, and ancient hymns of praise from the psalms to the music of "Mary, Look upon Us."] Can it be that this inventive liturgical misuse of melodies has been added to the proposed new liturgical materials as P.R., a public relations move intended to placate those of the faithful who love those melodies but do not realize that it is inappropriate to use them thus? That is, is there a strategy here to play upon sentimental attachment to those melodies to win popularity for the changes?

---

[369] Orlando di Lasso (Roland de Lassus, 1532-1594), *Missa ad imitationem moduli "Susanne un jour," für funfstimmigen gemischten Chor*, ed. Siegfried Hermelink (Cassel: Bärenreiter, 1964), Chor-Archiv, No. 4388. Excerpted from Orlando di Lasso, *Sämtliche Werke, Neue Reihe*. Band 4: Messen 10-17, ed. Seigfried Hermelink (Cassel: Bärenreiter, 1964), No. 3404.

[370] J. S. Shedlock, "The Maltreatment of Music," *Proceedings of the Musical Association*, 10ᵗʰ Session, 1883-1884, pp. 95-123 at p. 97.

Or is it simply that changes are being made with increasingly little regard to the traditions of the Ruthenian Liturgy?

Original Conclusion

The Slavonic Liturgy deserves to be respected. We are stewards of the Liturgy, called to preserve it authentically. The faithful need and deserve this; the Catholic Church as a whole needs its Eastern lung to be sound; and our sister Orthodox Churches have a claim on our upholding the traditions we share with them.

In the entire liturgy of March 25, 2005, not one page, indeed scarcely one line of music or of text was free of change. If the entire worship of the faithful, every service, year-round, were to be altered so relentlessly, the faithful would bear the burden of implementing enormous changes. The time of transition would be long indeed. Moreover, the very notion of an all-encompassing set of liturgical changes to the text of the liturgy and to the texts of proper hymnody and to the music of the chants seems a voluntary Romanization, or perhaps a voluntary Americanization. Regrettably, the proposed recasting of the Divine Liturgy -- both in the version of October 12, 2004, and in the slightly revised version glimpsed since then -- "would distance the Byzantine-Ruthenian Catholic Metropolitan of Pittsburgh...both from the other Greek-Catholics in the United States and from Eastern Orthodox in the United States."[371]

Before any significant revision could be appropriately promulgated, much more work, wisdom, and prayer would be needed. Our responsibility is all the greater because both Greek and Slavonic underlie our Rite. An appropriate English translation of the entire Septuagint (at a minimum, the Psalter) and perhaps a new translation of the New Testament produced with cognizance of the Septuagint are needed. Ideally, full studies are also needed of how the Slavonic scriptures correlate with the Greek and of how and where the Slavonic scriptures match the Liturgy in diction and phrasing. In addition, analysis of Slavonic poetics and rhetoric are needed to clarify how the Slavonic renders the Greek, and also to indicate how the English ought to render the Slavonic.

---

[371] Keleher, *Response to the Proposed Recasting of the Byzantine-Ruthenian Liturgy* (as in note 6 above), 267.

Our hierarchs may judge from the response they received to the proposed revision introduced on March 25, 2005, whether the persons who had proposed the revisions had adequately advised them on what to expect, and why. One hopes that the expectations were not rooted in the patronizing attitude that the faithful and clergy were ignorant creatures of habit who might fuss, but would accept everything proposed.

The word "Theotokos" is an excellent focus here. From the analysis above of this beautiful and profound title for Mary, it is clear that the prior English translation of the Divine Liturgy had, in effect, Romanized it, rendering *Bohoróditsa* as "Mother of God." Especially for parishes that had not sustained any familiarity with the term *Bohoróditsa* in hymns, the phrase "Mother of God" would have been perhaps the beloved manner of referring to Our Lady. And elsewhere in the Metropolia the term "Godbearer," not "Theotokos," would have been prominent. Unless the parishes were hearing sermons using the term Theotokos, unless catechesis had regularly used it, why should anyone have expected that parishioners would welcome the introduction of a technical term in Greek? Even if the introduction of "Theotokos" had been the only change in the liturgy on March 25, 2005, it would have been pastorally insensitive to make the change without weeks of preparation.

Happily, it appears that at present very few textual changes are warranted. And, it is not clear yet that any musical changes are appropriate or that the ones intended are well-conceived. Theologically, musically, poetically, the materials that are superior are the ones already in many parishes, already familiar, already known by heart by many and inspiring to visitors. Given, then, that there is no real urgency to institute a revised liturgy, proper care can and should be taken to study the full Ruthenian recension and to proceed from there. Meanwhile, it is to be hoped that there will be advances in the dissemination of information about women in the Church.

Spokane, 2006

Epilogue

The revised Divine Liturgy became mandatory for The Byzantine Metropolitan Church *Sui Juris* of Pittsburgh, U.S.A., as of the Feast of SS. Peter and Paul, June 29, 2007. The official volume contains the liturgies for S. John Chrysostom and S. Basil the Great (pp. 11-103), as well as preparatory prayers (pp. 4-10), Great Vespers (pp. 104-22), the Sunday Eight Tones (pp. 123-63), the Pentecostarion (pp. 164-241), Immovable Feasts (pp. 242-357), Commons for Classes of Saints (pp. 358-405), Commons for the Days of the Week (pp. 406-13), Special Intentions (pp. 414-31), Panachida (pp. 432-49), a selection of ten liturgical and scriptural hymns (pp. 450-61), and a glossary (462-67). In the abstract, the assemblage of these materials in a modern, printed edition is a great desideratum.

In the fact, however, the revised *Divine Liturgy* retains the few virtues and the many problems of the draft discussed above. Fitting changes in text were revising "testament" to "covenant," "priesthood" to "presbyterate," and, in the irmos of the Annunciation, "ark" to "tabernacle." A most positive and appropriate revision is that the word "essence" is now in the Symbol of Faith (p. 51). For these changes the faithful may be lastingly grateful. Also, in one instance a legitimate concern raised by the faithful had effect upon the revisers of the *Divine Liturgy:* Happily and significantly, the phrase "God-loving" was not abandoned (p. 12). Four verbal improvements, however, amid countless changes form a small proportion.

With sorrow it must be noted that the many problems of the draft revision have become mandatory in the revised *Divine Liturgy*. It is rife with politically correct linguistic changes with a limited shelf date: in the Creed itself "for us men" has become "for us," and throughout the liturgy the "Lover of Mankind" has become the one who "loves us all."[372] Myriad alterations of music and text were promulgated. With disregard for the traditions of religious chant, the non-liturgical melody of "Mary, Look upon Us" has been presented as an authorized setting for liturgical texts and for ancient communion hymns from the Psalms.

Regarding women, the quick-fix ideological banishing of words such as "man" and "son" has taken place. The need remains for seminarians, catechists, and priests to be educated in the rich and positive Christian traditions regarding the spiritual equality of women, their achievements as ισαπόστολοι "equal to the apostles," the innovative and profoundly positive Christian interpretation of women as types of Christ in his Passion, and so much more.

The desiderata set forth in this volume and summarized in its conclusion remain desirable and needed. A new and excellent resource for study of the liturgical texts is the "Study Text of Translations of the Ruthenian Divine Liturgy of St. John Chrysostom," which has four columns. In adjacent columns are the authorized English translation that had been used in the Metropolia for forty years and the 2007 revised *Divine Liturgy*.[373]

In 2008 Archimandrite Robert F. Taft, S.J., expressed "consternation" about the "contemporary mania for 'liturgical creativity'" and in particular he decried the actions of some in "introducing [allegedly] on my authority changes into the liturgical service."[374] One must note that he does not identify the revised *Divine Liturgy* as being in

---

[372] "for us": p. 51; the one who "loves us all": e.g., p. 90.

[373] This public-access download -- DL-Chrysostom-Ruthenian-Study-Text-4-Review-20090406.pdf – was designed and created by John Vernoski for private study only, not for unauthorized liturgical celebration of the prior translation. The complex download requires Adobe Acrobat and it is available online at: http://www.byzcath.org/forums/ubbthreads.php/topics/317817/Study%20Text%20of%20the%20Ruthenian%20Di.

[374] Robert F. Taft, S.J., *A History of the Liturgy of St. John Chrysostom, Volume VI: The Communion, Thanksgiving, and Concluding Rites*, Orientalia Christiana Analecta 281 (Pontificio Instituto Orientale, 2008), p. 785. Promoters of the revised *Divine Liturgy* have frequently claimed Fr. Taft's authority and approval for that revision. Such claims appear to overstate both Fr. Taft's role and his assessment. His role may have been merely to verify that the revision did not contain heresy, so that nothing stood in the way of (*nihil obstat*) promulgating it. His assessment is, it would seem, well indicated by the comments quoted here.

his thoughts. Nonetheless his comments are direct, fitting, and timely. He affirms that "the liturgical tradition of a Church is a story of a people at prayer, the Church's ideal model of worship to which I must rise, not something I am invited to reduce to the level of my own banality."[375]

For the present, the hierarchs could graciously accede to the longing of many of the faithful to worship again in what had long been the accepted chant settings and texts, settings and texts which may in truth be more authentic to the Byzantine tradition than are the revised versions. Such an action by the Metropolia would do much to restore confidence in the modes of worship.

November 13, 2010
Feast of Saint John Chrysostom

---

[375] Taft, *Communion*, p. 786.

Indices

General Index

This index includes people, places, terms, first lines of texts, etc. Historical persons, biblical persons, scholars, and members of the hierarchy and laity are included. If a page number is followed by the letter "n" this means that the word in question is found in a footnote on that page.

Armenian sources, 76
Asmatikon, 87
assonance, 40
Athanasius, S., 30, 52
Augustine, St., 23-24

Baird, Mrs. Margaret, 40n, 48n
balanced representation of the sexes, 32-33
banality, xiv, 51, 58, 109
Baptism:
 of Jesus, 9
 the Sacrament, 23-24, 66
Barclay, William, 68n
Bartholomew I, Ecumenical Patriarch, 11
Basil M. Schott, O.F.M., Metropolitan of Pittsburgh, 14n, 60n
Basil of Caesarea, S. (also called Basil the Great), xvii, 62, 76, 107
Beatitudes, 53, 54, 56
beauty, beautiful, xvii, 2, 15, 39, 55, 56, 86, 100, 106
Benedict XVI, Pope, 7, 30, 77
Bermuda Triangle, 30
Bible, xiv, 6, 7, 22, 43, 51, 74, 76
Bible, English translations of 21
Bible, Greek: *See* Old Greek, Septuagint, Theodotion.
Bible, Latin Vulgate, 8, 10, 35, 36, 40, 76
Bible, Slavonic, 43, 74, 78
"Birth of God," xiv, 20, 22, 24
Bishop White Seminary at Gonzaga University, xi, 33n
Blackfriars Hall, Oxford University, xi, 33n
blessing, 13, 29, 50, 61, 70-71, 84, 90, 101, 103
Boh Predvičnyj ("Eternal God"), hymn, 97
Boh Sja Raždajet ("God's Son is Born"), hymn, 98
Bohorodice Djivo, hymn, 98, see also 93
Bohoróditsa, vi, xiv, 11, 15-18, 21-22, 24-25, 43, 59, 81, 106
Bokshai, Ioann V. and Iosif I. Malinich, 48, 85
Božaja Mati, Čísta Djívice ("Purest of Virgins"), Marian hymn, 99
Brescia Casket, 65n
Brock, Sebastian, 34m, 91
Brown, Raymond E., S.S., 68, 69n
Byzantine Book of Prayer (1995), 28, 81
Byzantine Catholic Archeparchy of Pittsburgh, vi, 2, 5, 15, 24, 44, 92, 105, 107
Byzantine Catholic Seminary of SS. Cyril and Methodius, Pittsburgh, 2, 3, 50, 91, 101
Byzantine lectionary, 76
Byzantine Metropolitan Church *Sui Juris* of Pittsburgh, vi, 2, 5, 15, 24, 44, 85, 92, 105, 107
 Council of Hierarchs, 14n, 38
Byzantine Seminary Press, 87, 99

Cabasilas, Nicholas, 78
calendar, church, 33, 52
Cappadocian Fathers, 31
Caragounis, Chrys C., 68n
Carpenter, Marjorie, 34n, 35n
Carpathian chant, xvii
    See also chant.
Casey, Maurice, 7n, 68n
catechesis, 4, 28, 44, 52, 79, 106, 108
Catechism of the Catholic Church, 12
Celestine I, Pope, 16
Cenae tuae (Vespers hymn, Great Thursday), 92
Centurion, 74
Chant, 29, 48, 50, 73, 80, 90, 91, 93, 100, 103, 109
    Byzantine / Greek, 14, 79, 87, 91, 93, 94n
    Carpathian chant, xvii
    Gregorian, 72, 87
    Hungarian, 85
    liturgical, 60, 92, 93, 94n, 95, 97, 99, 100, 101, 102, 105, 109
    melismatic, 86-87
    prostopinije = Plain, 85, 101
    Slavonic, 28, 43, 60, 72, 79, 85, 87, 88
    Tones, 93-95
    Tone 1, p. 87
    Tone 2, p. 48
    Tone 4, p. 14, 48
    Tone 7, p. 14, 48
chant-inspired vernacular compositions, 93-96
Cherubic Hymn, Cherubikon, 73, 92, 93, 95, 101, 103
    set to non-liturgical melody, 101, 103
cherubic posture, 12
cherubim, 10, 95, 96, 101
"children of God," 54
Chilton, Bruce D., 68n
Chrismation, 12, 24
"Christ is risen from the dead!" 74
Christos Pantocrator, 33
Christos Rodilsja; Boh Voplotilsja ("Rejoice All Nations"), 97, 100
Christ's volition, 57
Chrysostom, John, S., xvii, 1, 34, 76, 80, 107, 108, 109
church architecture, 75, 77
Clement of Alexandria, S., 52
Communion, 5, 8, 13, 78-79
    See also Eucharist.

115

Damasus, Pope, 36
d'Ancona, Alessandro, 34n
Daniel, biblical book of, xiii, 7, 8, 9, 68-69
Daniel, holy prophet, 9
Dante, 91
Decalogue, 75
Deferrari, Roy J., 77n
Demetrius of Antioch, 34
Di Lella, Alexander A., O.F.M., 8n, 9n, 68n, 69n
dignity, 39, 56
Dionysius bar Salībī, bishop of Amida, 34
Dismissal, 50, 86, 90
diversity, xiii, 2
divinization, 1, 31
 See also theosis.
Divnaja Novina ("Wondrous News"), Christmas song, 93-95, 97
Djivo Mati, Zastupaj Nas ("Virgin Mother, Intercessor"), Marian hymn, 99n
doctrine:
 Catholic and Orthodox, 4, 11, 19, 41, 57
 language and the accurate expression of doctrine, 17, 41
 of the Immaculate Conception, 20, 21, 57
 of the Incarnation, 19, 41, 53
 of the spiritual equality of the sexes, 1, 4, 32-33, 108
 of the Virgin Birth, 53
 of theosis, 1, 31, 47, 52, 55
Dormition, feast of, 16, 20
doxology, 89-90
The Drama of Susanna (Greek), 33n
dumbing down, xiv, 51, 87n, 89

Easter Troparion, 60, 74-75
Eastern Catholics, 1, 3, 5, 9, 14, 27, 30
Ecumenical Council of Constantinople (381), 11
Ecumenical Patriarch Bartholomew I, p. 11
ektene, 16, 56, 59, 64, 65
Elizabeth, words of, 16-17, 19, 32, 92, 93
Encounter, 53
Entrance into the Temple, Feast of, 16, 20
Ephrem the Syrian, 34n
"equal to the apostles," 33, 37, 45, 108
Eriugena, 24
"Essence," restored to the Creed, 67, 107
Esther, 33
eternal memory (*Vičnaja pamjat*), 29, 48
Ethiopian Church, 1

Marian Shrine of Marija Povč (Mary of Povch), 98
marriage, 66
"marriage supper of the Lamb," 1
Martha of Bethany, S., profession of faith, 32, 49, 65
Martyr, Justin, 6
martyrs, 62, 102
"Mary, Look upon Us" (*Prizji O Marije*), Marian hymn, 101-03, 108
Mary the Mother of God, 15-20, 22-23, 81, 83, 106. *See also* Magnificat.
    and "iconic character" of women, 84
    and theosis, 23-24
    Annunciation to, 18, 19, 82, 83-84, 94
    as Ark of the Covenant, 81-82
    as pure, 21, 53, 57
    as "sanctified Temple," 43
    as Theotokos, 15, 16
    as type of the Church, 23
    at the Crucifixion, 32
    Byzantine precursor to the "Hail, Mary," 92, 93n
    Dormition, 20
    Encounter / Presentation, 53
    Entrance into the Temple, 20
    finds Jesus in the Temple, 19, 54
    "Hail, Mary," 92, 93n
    Mother of Jesus, 19
    Nativity of Mary, Feast of, 20
    Protection of Mary, feast of, 99n
    Synaxis of Mary, December 26, p. 20
    Visitation, 17, 19
Mary of Povch, 98
Matrona of Perge, 63n
Maximos IV, Patriarch of Antioch, 1
Maximus the Confessor, 23, 52
melisma, 86-87
Melkite, 80
memory, 35, 37-39, 45, 58, 98
metaphor, 20, 38, 74
meter, metrical, 92-95, 97, 99-100
Methodius, bishop of Olympos, 23, 34
Metropolitan Cantor Institute (MCI), 53, 87, 90, 91
Metropolitan Isaiah, Greek Metropolis of Denver, 79-80
Metropolitan Nicholas of Amissos, 85
Mills, Rev. William C., 28n
Mitsakis, Kariophiles, 24n
Mohr, Joseph, 101
Mohrmann, Christine, 41

Monastery of St. Gregory Palamas in Perrysville, Ohio, 82n
monastic *acta*, 63
Morgan, J. R., 63n
Moses, 62, 75
"Mother of God," 15, 16, 17, 18, 19, 22, 23, 81, 106
Mount Saint Macrina (Sisters of St. Basil the Great), Uniontown, Pennsylvania, 99
Mount Tabor Byzantine Catholic Monastery, Redwood Valley, California, 36n
Münz-Manor, Ophir, 34n
Munificentissimus Deus (1950), 84
music, xiii, 2, 3, 5, 13, 27, 28, 29, 35, 40, 47, 48, 49, 53, 59, 60, 70-72, 73, 79, 82, 85-103, 105, 106, 108
Musurillo, Herbert, 34n
Myrrhbearing women, Sunday of, 52n
mystery, 14, 17, 20, 21, 24, 43, 51, 52, 53, 67, 78, 79, 81
    See also Sacrament / Mystery.

Nativity, Feast of, Fourth Sticheron for Great Compline, 84
Nebo I Zeml'a ("Heaven and Earth"), Christmas hymn, 97, 98, 100
New Feminism, xiv, 55
Newman, Barclay M., Jr., 74n
Nicene Council, 67
Nicene Creed, 11, 41, 67
Nicholas of Amissos, Metropolitan, 85
Nicodemus Hymns, 87n
Noah's Ark, 59
"The noble Joseph…," 89-90
Nonnos, bishop, 63n
Nova Radost' Stala ("Joyful News"), Christmas hymn, 93, 94-95, 97

"O Godbearer Virgin," 81
"O Joyful Light," 60, 70-72
O Marije Mati Vsich, Marian hymn, 100n
"O Theotokos Virgin," 81
Old Greek (Bible), xiv, 8
    See also Septuagint.
Old Latin (Bible), 8, 44
"One is Holy," 8, 78-79
ordination, 61
Orientale Lumen (1995), 30, *see also* 1, 2, 31.
Orientalium Ecclesiarum (1895), 30
Origen, 6, 7, 76
orthodox, orthodoxy, 19, 23, 57, 66, 76
Orthodox Churches, 19, 24, 27, 28, 30, 55, 63, 80, 85, 86, 90, 96, 105
Orthodox Metropolitan of Amissos, 85
"orthodox," the word, 57

Otče naš (Our Father), 59
Otwinowski, Erazm, 95
Our Father, xiv, 13, 65, 93
Our Father, in Slavonic, 59
Our Father, set to non-liturgical melody, 101
Oxford University, xi, 33

Palonniki Uniontowns'ki ("Come to Uniontown"), Marian hymn, 99, 100
parables, 32
  parable of the sower, 75
  parable of the vineyard, 9n
  parable of the woman who finds the lost coin, 33-34
paradox, 53
paraliturgical music, 95, 100, 101, 102, 103, 105, 108
parallel, parallelism, 9, 20, 40, 48, 50, 60, 69, 74, 77
Paretsky, Albert, O.P., 9n
Pascha, 12-13, 29, 33, 97
"Pascha," the word, 10, 41, 42, 43
paschal katabasia, 53
paschal stichera, 42
Paschal Troparion, 75
Passover, 42, 43, 81
Pataki, Andrew, bishop, 11, 13
Paul, St., 52, 65, 107
Peredera, Anatoli, 82n, 84n
Perrysville, Ohio, Monastery of St. Gregory Palamas, 82n
Peter, St., profession of faith, 32, 49n, 66
Petras, David, Fr., 13
Petro, Rev. John G., 85n
Phos Hilaron, 60, 70-72
Photina, S. (lit. "Enlightened Woman"), 33
pietism, 27n
Pittsburgh, Byzantine Catholic Seminary of SS. Cyril and Methodius, 2, 3, 50, 91, 101
Pius IX, Pope, *Ineffabilis Deus* (1854), 20n
Pius XII, Pope, *Munificentissimus Deus* (1950), 84
Pod Tvoju Milost', Marian hymn, 100n
Pod tvoj pokrov, Marian hymn, 99n
Podskalsky, Gerhard, 16n
poem, poetry, xiii, 3, 14, 27, 32, 34, 35, 40-42, 47, 51, 54, 56, 70-72, 90- 95, 97-99, 105, 105
Pokorsky, Rev. Jerry, 66n
Poland, 30, 66
Polish biblical poetry, 95
political correctness, 70
Pontifical Council for Promoting Christian Unity, 11-12

126

Roman Missal, Third Edition, 66n
Roman Synod of Pope Celestine, 16
Romanization, 6, 18, 105
Romanos the Melode, 34, 35n
rubrics, 49-50
Russell, Jeffrey Burton, xi, xii-xv
Russian culture, 102
Russian Orthodox, 82, 84
Russian Orthodox Church of Saint Jonah of Manchuria, in North Houston, Texas, 82, 84n
Ruth, 33
Ruthenian, Ruthenian Church, xiii, 1, 2, 5, 21, 28, 29, 37, 39, 52, 64, 83, 88, 91, 98, 102, 105
Ruthenian recension, 44, 106

Sacrament / Mystery, 24, 51, 53, 66
Sacrosanctum Concilium (1964), 15
St. Albert Institute for Catholic Thought, 32n
Saint Elias Church, Eparchy of Toronto, 63n
St. Peter's Basilica, Vatican, 85
salvation, 20, 24, 58, 64, 68, 73, 83, 84
Samaritan Woman, 33n
sanctification, 13, 31, 42-43, 52, 78, 79, 83
    See also theosis, deification.
sanctuary, 77-78, 80
Schism, 1
Schmalstieg, William R., 21n, 42n, 61n, 72n, 75n
Schott, Basil M., O.F.M., Metropolitan of Pittsburgh, 14n, 60n
Schultze, David Henry, 34n
Second Vatican Council (1962-1965), 2, 36, 37
seminarians, 4, 108
Septuagint, xiv, 1, 4, 5-10, 11, 17, 18, 23, 36, 68, 69, 75, 76, 82, 105
sermons, 22, 32, 34, 53, 78, 106
sexes, 9, 32-35, 84
Shedlock, J. S., 103n
Shereghy, Basil, 13
shroud, 89-90
Siegenthaler, David, 93n
"Silent Night," 101
Simeon, 32
Skurla, William C., Bishop of Van Nuys, 60n
slava, 39, 95
Slavonic, Slavic (church, language, rite), xiii, 1, 3, 4, 5, 10-11, 13, 15, 16, 17, 20, 21, 22, 24, 25, 27, 29, 37, 39, 41, 42, 43, 44, 45, 49, 51, 53, 55, 56, 57, 58, 59, 60, 61, 64, 70, 74, 76, 79, 81, 82, 83, 85, 92, 96, 97, 105
Slavonic chant, 28, 43, 60, 72, 79, 85, 87, 88

Slavonic hymns, 27-28, 35
    Christmas songs, 97-98
    communion, 97
    Marian, 21, 98-100
    other, 70-72, 91, 101-02
    paraliturgical, nonliturgical, 4, 93, 95, 98, 100-03
    See also individual titles.
Solomon, 62
Son of Man, 67-70
"sons of men," 54
Špidlík, Tomáš, S.J., Cardinal, 52
spiritual autonomy, 66
spiritual equality of the sexes, 1, 4, 32-33, 108
Spokane, Washington, Byzantine Catholic Church of SS. Cyril and Methodius, xi, 4, 85
Stamford, Connecticut, Catholic Eparchy of, 6, 80
Sticheron, stichera, 42, 48, 72, 84. *See also* Apostichera.
Strasti, 15n, 60n, 97
style, 38-40, 45, 51, 86, 99
"substance," in translating the Creed, 67
suppression of the masculine generic, 53-55, 102n
Susanna, 9, 33
"*Svjat, svjat, svjat*" (communion hymn), 95-96
Symbol of Faith, Symbolum, vi, 68, 69
Symeon of Thessalonika, 78
Symeon the New Theologian, 52
synagogue, 77
Synaxis of Mary, 20
syntax, 38, 40, 43, 55
Syriac, 7, 34
    See also Ephrem the Syrian, Jacob of Serug, Zachariah of Mitylene.

Tabernacle of God, as title for Mary, 20, 81
Taft, Robert F., S.J., Archimandrite, 6, 12, 44, 49, 63, 78, 80, 108-09
Taube, Moshe, 1n
Temple, 16, 19, 20, 32, 43, 54, 77
"testament," vi, 3, 4, 47, 75-78, 107
Tetragrammaton, 17
"That we may receive the King of all,"
    set to non-liturgical melody, 101
    translation, 73
Thekla, 33n
Theodoret, 62n, 63n
Theodotion-Daniel, 8, 9
theogenesia, "birth of God," 23

Wedding:
- Actual: see Crowning
- at Cana, 84
- image of soul's union with Christ, 12

Wesche, Kenneth Paul, 55n

Westernizing, 22. *See also* Americanization, Romanization.

Whitehead, Kenneth D., 36n

widow of Zarephath, 33

William C. Skurla, Bishop of Van Nuys, 60n

women, xiv, 9, 31-35, 84, 85, 102, 106, 108
- as types of Christ, 33
- "equal to the apostles,"
- holy women's words, 31
- holy women at the tomb, 31, 33
- in the Greek Old Testament, more positive than in Hebrew, 9
- integral to Church, 4
- interacting with Jesus, 32
- myrrhbearing, 52n
- sermons on, 35
- spiritual equality, 1, 4, 32, 33
- *See also* specific biblical women and female saints: Anna, Conception of Anne, Elizabeth, Esther, Eve, Holy Women at the Tomb, Jairus' daughter, Jephthah's daughter, Judith, Martha of Bethany, Mary the Mother of God, Matrona of Perge, Photina, Ruth, Samaritan woman, Susanna, Thekla, widow of Zarephath. Also, parable of the woman who finds the lost drachma.

word play, word echo:
- on "confined … is   confined" (*zatvorjajetsja…zatvorivyj*), 53
- on "creation" and "created," 72
- on "creature … Creator" (*sozdanija… Sozdatel'*), 53
- on "*skvernych. … že v'irnych*," 82
- on "sun" and "Son," 14
- on "word" (*slovo*) and "Word" (*Slovo*), 14

"worship, rational" 67

Zachariah of Mitylene, 64n

Word Indices:

Greek

ἀγαπητός / ἀγαπητή, 9
ἅγια τοῖς ἁγίοις, Τὰ, 79
ἅγιος..., Εἷς, 79
αἵματι Διαθήκης, 76
αἰωνίου, 76
ἄνθρωπος, 68, 69
apocalypsis, 41
ἀχειροπόητα, 13
ἄχραντα, 20

γενέσθαι, 18
γίγνομαι, 18, 19
γονεῖς, 19
γύναι, 84

Δείπνου σου, Τοῦ, 92
δι' ἡμᾶς τοὺς ἀνθρώπους, 69
διαθηκη, 75
διαθηκην καινην, 75
το δραμα της Σωσαννιδο (*The Drama of Susanna*), 33n

εγω ειμι, 18
ἐγὼ πεπιστευκα, 66
εικονα, 34
Εἷς ἅγιος..., 79
ἐν γαστρί ἕξει καὶ τέξεται ὁ υἱόν, 18
ensarkosis, 41
ἔτεκεν τον υἱόν, 18

131

Hebrew and Aramaic

Latin

anima, 55
animus, 55
caritas, 55
Cenae tuae, 92
cor, 55

Dei Genetrix, 17
Deipara, xiv, 17
Deus, 20n, 55, 84
dilectio, 55
Domine, 55
Dominus exercituum, 10

Filioque, 3, 11-12, 24

glorificare, gloriare, 41

immaculata, 20
incarnatio, 41

Mater Dei, xiv, 17
mens, 55

novum testamentum, 76

Omnipotens aeterne Deus, 55

pasci, 55
Pater, 55

revelatio, 41

salvatio, 64
salvum fac, 10
Sancta sanctis, 60, 78
satiari, 55
spiritus, 55
sumere, 55

Slavonic

Other Languages

Anglo-Saxon:
>   *ungewemmed*, 20

Aztec:
>   *tilma*, 14

French:
>   *salut*, 64

English Words in the Liturgy

Scriptural Index:

Old Testament

New Testament

Catherine Brown Tkacz

Dr. Catherine Brown Tkacz has been publishing on the history of Christianity for three decades. The first woman to earn the Ph.D. in Medieval Studies from the University of Notre Dame, she has served as managing editor of *The Oxford Dictionary of Byzantium* and as a program officer for the National Endowment for the Humanities. Currently Research Associate for the Bishop White Seminary at Gonzaga University, she was recently visiting faculty at Blackfriars Hall at Oxford University, lecturing on the Theotokos and the Incarnation. Her research on biblical studies and theology have appeared in such journals as *Saint Vladimir's Theological Quarterly*, *Vigiliae Christianae*, *Studia Patristica*, *Gregorianum*, *Catholic Biblical Quarterly*, and *Recherches de Théologie et Philosophie Médiévales*.